THORA HIRD'S
PRAISE BE! YEARBOOK

Elizabeth Gort has worked with Thora on **Praise Be!** for fifteen years, first as a BBC Television producer, and, for the past four years, as an independent writer and broadcaster.

They share the same birthday and have become close friends.

THORA HIRD'S

Praise Be!

YEARBOOK

Thora Hird
and Elizabeth Gort

Fount
An Imprint of HarperCollinsPublishers

First published in Great Britain in 1991 by Fount Paperbacks
Fount is an imprint of
HarperCollinsReligious
part of HarperCollins Publishers
77–85 Fulham Palace Road, London W6 8JB

Typeset by Medcalf Type Ltd, Bicester, Oxon
Printed and bound in Great Britain by
Cox & Wyman Ltd, Reading, Berks

CONTENTS

INTRODUCTION

When I wrote my *Praise Be! Notebook* last year, I hoped it would be a way of repaying the kindness of people who have been sending me such lovable letters over the past 15 years on **Praise Be!** I feel so unhappy when I find it impossible to reply to all your letters personally, or give everyone a mention on the programme. So I thought – a little collection of some of my favourite stories, thoughts, prayers, poems and hymns would be my way of saying a very loving "thank you".

When the *Notebook* went into its fifth reprint after only a few months, I realized I'd better get my skates on and write another little volume – before your next lot of **Praise Be!** letters arrived.

So here it is, and I've called it my *Praise Be! Yearbook*, because this collection is mainly about things that have become part of the warp and woof of Scotty's and my life at different times of the year. For instance, one of my childhood boasts, to the admiration and envy of all my school-friends, was that our family birthdays all fell in consecutive months: Mother in April, Thora in May, Father in June, my sister Olga in July, and our Neville in August. I took pride in that – as though I had personally arranged it! I think even Scotty wonders if I married him because his birthday is in September!

As well as birthdays and anniversaries, there are those lovely, simple things every year, like when Jan makes a dramatic entrance into our cottage early on an April morning, and before she needs say a word, Scotty and

I both look up from our breakfast and say together: "Is it the first cuckoo?", and we all go out into the garden and listen. It never loses its wonder, and grows more precious, the older we get.

For all my fifteen years of presenting **Praise Be!** my friend and co-writer, Elizabeth Gort, has always been my right-hand woman. We have long preparation sessions each year, when she comes round for lunch with Scotty and me, bringing with her a great pile of VHS cassettes of the past year's *Songs of Praise*. We get out all the letters, and work on ideas for the next series. It takes several days, because we spend so much time laughing, and Scotty has to keep reminding us to "get on with it!". Now she has helped me prepare this *Praise Be! Yearbook*, and it's been like working with family, and we've loved every minute of it.

Of course, I've also included more of our favourite songs of praise, ones that capture the mood of the changing seasons, and praise the Lord; and many more prayers, poems and thoughts from the **Praise Be!** post-bag. Thank you for sending them to me. Now I send them back to you, all collected together, with my love.

THORA HIRD, *May 1991*

Winter

Happy New Year!
You don't have to stay up late on a winter night to see
bright starlit skies. At any time after tea you can look out
of your window, or better still, step out of doors into the
darkness and look up at the moon and stars. Like the
person who wrote this traditional American carol, it
always sets me wondering . . .

I Wonder as I Wander

I wonder as I wander, out under the sky,
How Jesus the Saviour did come for to die
For poor or'n'ry people like you and like I . . .
I wonder as I wander, out under the sky.

When Mary bore Jesus, 'twas in a cow's stall,
With wise men and animals and shepherds and all.
But high from the heavens a star's light did fall,
And the promise of ages it then did recall.

If Jesus had wanted for any wee thing,
A star in the sky or a bird on the wing,
Or all of God's angels in heaven for to sing
He could surely have had it, 'cause he was the King.

I wonder as I wander, out under the sky,
How Jesus the Saviour did come for to die

For poor or'n'ry people like you and like I . . .
I wonder as I wander, out under the sky.

North Carolina traditional carol

January

As soon as the Christmas and New Year seasons are over, all the cards come down, joy though it is to receive them, with their loving messages and news from old friends.

I've always been a bit tidy, I have to admit. And I'm not trying to swank – honestly! I enjoy dusting and polishing beautiful things, wood and glass and china ornaments, or buffing up the brass to a bright shine.

I'm not as bad as my Auntie Lizzie. Have I told you about her? She was so house-proud, she would even brush the dust off the coal before she put it on the fire! I'm not kidding you. She had a big, deep-set fireplace with a white hearthstone, which she always kept scrubbed and smoothed with a white rubbing stone. She used to have a royal stand-back of a fire, and when she lifted more coal up in the tongs, bits of black coal dust would fall on her white grate. Well she wasn't having that! So she kept a little brush by the coal scuttle, and every time she lifted out a lump of coal, she would brush the dust off over the scuttle – do you follow? – before putting it onto the fire. I remember my mother's face as she watched this performance, and her saying, ''Well, Lizzie, now I've seen everything!''

I just have to think of my Auntie Lizzie to get into character for my part of Edie, putting down newspapers every time anyone comes into her kitchen in *Last of the Summer Wine*!

I don't know who wrote this next little prayer-poem,

but I think they must have had people like Auntie and me in mind!

Lord of all pots and pans and things, since I've no time
   to be
A saint by doing lovely things or watching late with Thee,
Or dreaming in the dawn-light or storming heaven's
   gates,
Make me a saint by getting meals, and washing up the
   plates.

Although I must have Martha's hands, I have a Mary
   mind:
And when I black the boots and shoes, Thy sandals, Lord,
   I find,
I think of how they trod the earth, each time I scrub the
   floor;
Accept this meditation, Lord, I haven't time for more.

Warm all the kitchen with Thy love, and light it with Thy
   peace;
Forgive me all my worrying, and make my grumbling
   cease.
Thou, who dids't love to give men food, in room or by
   the sea,
Accept this service that I do – I do it unto Thee.

Anon

The weeks after Christmas can be a difficult time for people, and I've noticed that we often find ourselves visiting old friends in hospital in early January. I just can't tell you how much it meant to me, getting all your cards, letters and flowers when I was in hospital myself in January having a heart by-pass. There were so many, I don't think I'll be able to answer them all, but please know I am so grateful.

I remember years ago, when I was in the Royal Lancaster Infirmary, after a rather unfortunate road accident. I won't go into details now, but suffice it to say that I ended up in hospital with a face thirteen and a half inches wide – three times the size it should have been. A lady came to visit her niece in the next bed. She saw me and did a double take. She came over and whispered in my ear, very loudly: "Oh, I say! Is it Thora? It is, in't it? Oh what a sight! What a sample! What a good job you were never good looking before!"

Now I know Lancashire women, and I know she intended that very kindly!

> Unless the Lord keepeth the city
> the watchman waketh in vain.
>
> Psalm 127: verse 2

It's funny how quiet some parts of London can be at the beginning of January. I suppose everyone must be at the January Sales. Well, I say "January" sales – they seem to start earlier and earlier each year. In fact, I believe they've started calling them "Pre-Christmas Sales"!

You get the chance to see what a beautiful city London really is. When the trees are bare you can see the houses better.

I like to think of January as the beginning of something new, not a hang-over from the year before. I always buy a little bunch of snowdrops as soon as they appear on the barrows in London, and I always used to bring them home to Jan when she was a little girl, and I loved seeing her face. Even when she lived in America, I used to ring her up as soon as they appeared and say, "The snowdrops are back on the barrows, Jan." Aren't snowdrops a special bit of the Lord's magic for us in the dark days of winter?

The Snowdrop

Close to the sod
There can be seen
A thought of God
In white and green.
Unmarred, unsoiled
It cleft the clay,
Serene, unspoiled
It views the day.

It is so holy
And yet so lowly,
Would you enjoy
Its grace and dower
And not destroy
The living flower?
Then you must, please,
Fall on your knees.

Anna Bunston de Bary

I usually make my first "appeal" in January for the next series of **Praise Be!** inviting viewers to choose and tell me about their favourite hymns from *Songs of Praise*. It's nice, because I know that soon afterwards your letters will start to arrive, and work can begin. Some old **Praise Be!** hands have started to jump the gun, and I get requests before I've been on television to ask for them.

Rather like those first little snowdrops that appear on a frosty January morning, these early letters have to brave the snowy wastes of an unprepared BBC postal department – and the Viewers' Correspondence Section!

Early or late, all your requests are taken into account, and the hymns we include are the ones that have been most asked for, or ones with perhaps just one or two people in mind, where we can all share their story. Like this one, from Linda Majhu in Wolverhampton:

Dear Thora,
Please could you play a hymn for my parents, Marjorie and Geoffrey Gould. When my father retired six years ago they moved into a "Granny Flat" at our house, so that my husband and I could look after them in their retiring years.

But sadly my husband died suddenly of a brain haemorrhage at the age of thirty-five. My daughter was 5 and I was expecting my second child.

I have gone back to work, and instead of being looked after, Mum and Dad have ended up looking after my two daughters. What would I have done without their love and support?

If possible, could we hear "Meekness and Majesty" by Graham Kendrick? It will remind us of all our holidays at Spring Harvest, Minehead.

Best wishes from Linda Majhu.

I visited Spring Harvest recently, Linda. What a cracking atmosphere there is, isn't there? And I had a lovely chat with Graham Kendrick about all the hymns he writes.

Meekness and Majesty

Meekness and Majesty,
Manhood and Deity,
In perfect harmony,
The man who is God.
Lord of eternity
Dwells in Humanity,
Kneels in humility –
And washes out feet.

Oh, what a mystery,
Meekness and majesty,
Bow down and worship,
For this is your God.

Father's pure radiance,
Perfect in innocence,
Yet learns obedience
To death on a cross.
Suffering to give us life,
Conquering through sacrifice;
And as they crucify
Prays: Father, forgive.
   Oh, what a mystery

Wisdom unsearchable,
God the invisible;

Love indestructible
In frailty appears.
Lord of infinity
Stooping so tenderly
Lifts our humanity
To the heights of His throne.
 Oh, what a mystery

Graham Kendrick

How far is it to Bethlehem?
Not very far . . .

Well – not if you happen to be a shepherd, it isn't. But what about the three wise men, whom we sing about after Christmas, at Epiphany?

The shepherds, who probably weren't very wise at all, had only to walk down the hill where they were standing and into the nearest town to find Jesus. But it's two weeks later before the Three Wise Men arrive, after travelling for miles and miles following a star – I don't think they would have appreciated anyone saying to *them* that it wasn't very far to Bethlehem! Far or near, clever-heads or simple folk, we are all welcome at the stable in Bethlehem, with our gifts and our burdens.

O Worship the Lord

O worship the Lord in the beauty of holiness!
Bow down before him, his glory proclaim;
With gold of obedience, and incense of lowliness,
Kneel and adore him, the Lord is his name!

Low at his feet lay thy burden of carefulness,
High on his heart he will bear it for thee,
Comfort thy sorrows, and answer thy prayerfulness,
Guiding thy steps as may best for thee be.

Fear not to enter his courts in the slenderness
Of the poor wealth thou wouldst reckon as thine:
Truth in its beauty, and love in its tenderness,
These are the offerings to lay on his shrine.

These, though we bring them in trembling and
    fearfulness,
He will accept for the name that is dear:
Mornings of joy give for evenings of tearfulness,
Trust for our trembling and hope for our fear.

O worship the Lord in the beauty of holiness!
Bow down before him, his glory proclaim;
With gold of obedience, and incense of lowliness,
Kneel and adore him, the Lord is his name!

J. S. B. Monsell (1811–75)

February

Seventy days before Easter is called Septuagesima. The only person I know who could get a word like that into a poem is our late, much lamented poet laureate, John Betjeman. Here's part of it.

Septuagesima

Septuagesima – time of waiting,
Running the race or holding fast.
Let's praise the man who goes to light
The church stove on an icy night.
Let's praise that hard-worked he or she
The Treasurer of the P.C.C.
Let's praise the cleaner of the aisles,
The nave and candlesticks and tiles.
Let's praise the organist who tries
To make the choir increase in size,
Or if that simply cannot be,
Just to improve its quality.
Let's praise the ringers in the tower
Who come to ring in cold and shower.
But most of all, let's praise the few
Who are seen in their accustomed pew
Throughout the year, whate'er the weather,
That they may worship God together.
These, like a fire of glowing coals,

Strike warmth into each other's souls,
And though they be but two or three
They keep the Church for you and me.

from "Septuagesima" by John Betjeman
Poems in the Porch

I do hope you haven't "grown out of" keeping St
Valentine's Day on 14 February, have you? Oh, I think
it's beautiful to have a special Saint's day for love. I enjoy
making old-fashioned Valentine cards like the Victorians
did, and writing sentimental verses inside. I often buy
bundles of turquoise and pink lace, which you can still
find on little market stalls up north. No, I don't send them
anonymously to some "leading man". I give them to
Daisy, James, Jan and Scotty, with my love!

One of my hobbies is drying and pressing flowers, and
I use them, too, for my Valentine cards. And I like to write
little "thoughts" for the person I'm giving them to. Well,
it gives me pleasure, and I'm harming nobody!

I think it makes a nice, special, loving gift, something
that you've made with your own fair hands, don't you?
Sometimes people send me little embroidered
bookmarks, and one lady, over eighty years old, has sent
me the most beautiful little hand-stitched needle case, that
she'd worked herself, which I just love to look at as well
as use. I wrote to her "You cannot *know* what pleasure
it gives me" – and I meant it.

As the days lengthen
The cold strengthens

Weather proverb

Very often – down in Sussex anyway – we find that
winter doesn't really get going until February. January
days can be beautifully mild and balmy, the evenings
growing gradually lighter, and I start to think 'Oh,
spring's just around the corner', and pop outside to look
for signs of life in the garden. I find them, too: snowdrops
and crocuses and tiny aconites, and pin-pricks of green
and red on the old trees. The birds are all singing cheerily
and dive-bomb us for bits. Scotty and I have always put
food out for the birds in winter.

Then suddenly Wham! The ground sets solid, the sky
lowers, and turns leaden, the starving birds are silent,
and an icy wind finds its way through holes and cracks
around the windows and doors that we didn't know
existed. I sometimes wonder if I'll ever feel warm again!
It can go on day after day for weeks.

Like all those people one February who sang their *Songs
of Praise* in the hot Spanish sunshine on a beach at
Benidorm, Scotty and I try when we can to make
February the month when we go away on our travels.

May the road rise to meet you,
May the wind be always at your back,
May the sun shine warm upon your face,
The rains fall soft upon your fields and,
Until we meet again,
May God hold you in the palm of his hand.

Irish Blessing (traditional)

The year I was having my hip operations done we were lucky enough to be able to visit Jerusalem. Now I realize it's a bit daft to think to yourself "He must have walked along this very road, over these very stones . . ." because since Jesus' time, I suppose a mere few million other people must have also walked along "that very road, over those very stones", and most of them thinking the same thing!

And yet, anyone who has been to the Holy Land will know what I'm talking about. Only time separates you from what happened in the Bible. People, landscape and buildings all look exactly the same as you've always pictured them.

For me the most moving part of our visit was when I went into the tiny cave where they say Jesus was born. I wouldn't know whether this *was* the stable or not. But if you ask me did I think it was – well, I did.

I often get letters on **Praise Be!** from viewers who have been to the Holy Land, too, sometimes on pilgrimages arranged, not by their church, but by their local radio stations. They can do wonderful work for the community, local radio stations, you know, getting people to talk to one another on phone-ins about local issues, arranging concerts and festivals, charity functions, and, as in this case, pilgrimages.

For many pilgrims the best part of the whole experience has been crossing the Sea of Galilee in a little boat, stopping in the middle, surrounded by the hills and mountains where Jesus prayed, and there, with the boat's engines turned off, singing Whittier's hymn "Dear Lord and Father of mankind".

Dear Lord and Father of Mankind

Dear Lord and Father of mankind,
Forgive our foolish ways!
Reclothe us in our rightful mind,
In purer lives thy service find,
In deeper reverence praise.

In simple trust like theirs who heard,
Beside the Syrian sea,
The gracious calling of the Lord,
Let us, like them, without a word
Rise up and follow thee.

O Sabbath rest by Galilee!
O calm of hills above,
Where Jesus knelt to share with thee
The silence of eternity,
Interpreted by love!

Drop thy still dews of quietness,
Till all our strivings cease;
Take from our souls the strain and stress,
And let our ordered lives confess
The beauty of thy peace.

Breathe through the heats of our desire
Thy coolness and thy balm;
Let sense be dumb, let flesh retire;
Speak through the earthquake, wind, and fire,
O still small voice of calm!

                    J. G. Whittier (1807–92)

God is a little lamb, you say. 'Tis true.
How helps you this unless you're his lamb too?

            Angelus Silesius (Johan Scheffler, 1624–77)

When we get home again at the end of February, there's often snow on the ground. And when we go down to the cottage in Sussex, the early lambs are out in the fields with their mothers. Sometimes in the afternoons they have "lamb races", when they leave their mothers for a few moments to race one another round and round the fields, tearing along, bucking and dancing, their long tails windmilling at the end of their fragile little bodies, and under their tiny galloping hooves the snowy ground glows pink in the setting sun.

The Lamb

Little lamb, who made thee,
Dost thou know who made thee,
Gave thee life and bade thee feed
By the stream and o'er the mead;
Gave thee clothing of delight,
Softest clothing, woolly, bright;
Gave thee such a tender voice,
Making all the vales rejoice?
Little lamb, who made thee?
Dost thou know who made thee?

Little lamb, I'll tell thee;
Little lamb, I'll tell thee:
He is called by thy name,
For He calls Himself a Lamb.
He is meek, and He is mild,
He became a little child.
I a child and thou a lamb,
We are called by His name.
Little Lamb, God bless thee!
Little Lamb, God bless thee!

William Blake

When we can't get away in February, and of course we can't always manage it, there's nothing like toasting your toes by a roaring log fire, and muffins taste different and better if you use an old-fashioned toasting fork! (No, I know you can't eat muffins without getting butter down your chin – who's worrying?) Another thing we like to

do for a treat is to give ourselves a "taste of summer".
On a particularly depressing February day, we go to the
deep freeze and take out a summer pudding that Scotty
made with fruit from the garden the summer before.
Heaven!

We don't have an open hearth in our home, but when
we go round to Jan's to catch up with the family news,
there's always a blazing log fire going for us in her ingle-
nook. When Daisy and James are home I sometimes look
at their faces bright in the firelight, and at Jan and
William, and my Scotty, and I realize how lucky and
fortunate I really am. I've got so many blessings to thank
"Him Upstairs" for, you know, and I do.

This next hymn says it all. I first remember hearing it
sung on *Songs of Praise* from Guernsey. They chose it
because it was the last hymn they'd been singing in the
Methodist church before the German invasion. When
they opened the church up again after the war, the
number was still up on the hymn board, so they sang
it again!

> How good is the God we adore!
> Our faithful, unchangeable friend:
> His love is as great as his power
> And knows neither measure nor end.
>
> For Christ is the first and the last;
> His Spirit will guide us safe home:
> We'll praise him for all that is past
> And trust him for all that's to come.
>
> J. Hart (1712–68)

Spring

The year's at the spring,
And days's at the morn;
Morning's at seven;
The hill-side's dew-pearled;
The lark's on the wing;
The snail's on the thorn;
God's in His heaven –
All's right with the world!

from "Pippa Passes"
by Robert Browning (1812–89)

March

Oh, I walk tall in March! The green daffodil shoots have yellow buds, swifts are arriving, we all put our clocks forward – isn't life suddenly better when we have light evenings? – and, best of all, the **Praise Be!** letters start to arrive.

It would be rather easy for me to get quite conceited when I read some of the kind, flattering things you write to me, so I always remember this little poem, in case I start to walk *too* tall!

Time to Think

Some time when you're feeling important,
Some time when your ego's in bloom,
Some time when you take it for granted
You're the best qualified one in the room,
Some time when you feel that your going
Would leave an unfillable hole –
Just follow these simple instructions,
And see how they humble your soul:

Take a bucket and fill it with water,
Put your hands in it up to your wrists,
Pull them out – and the hole which you see there
Is the measure of how you'd be missed!
The moral is really quite simple –

Just do the best that you can,
Be proud of yourself, but remember –
There is no indispensable man!

Anon

Or woman!

Some of your letters to **Praise Be!** in very simple words,
draw such a vivid picture of a person, or a way of life,
that I am often moved to tears.

> Dear Thora,
> Could you include the hymn "Mine Eyes have seen
> the Glory" for my husband John Shaw, who will
> be ninety-seven in September, and whose sight has
> gone these past seven years?
>   He was a man of the soil – a farmer – and now
> I must explain the growth in the fields to him.
>   Thank you.
>   Isabelle C. S. Shaw

I hope you are reading this now, Isabelle, as I was sorry
not to be able to include your request on the programme.
For you and John, here at least are the words, in the full
version, of that marvellous song:

Battle Hymn of the Republic

Mine eyes have seen the glory of the coming of the Lord:
He is trampling out the vintage where the grapes of wrath
   are stored;

He hath loosed the fateful lightning of his terrible swift
   sword:
> His truth is marching on.

I have seen Him in the watch-fires of a hundred circling
   camps:
They have builded Him an altar in the evening dews and
   damps;
I can read His righteous sentence by the dim and flaring
   lamps.
> His day is marching on.

I have read a fiery gospel, writ in burnished rows of steel:
"As ye deal with my contemners, so with you my grace
   shall deal;
Let the Hero, born of woman, crush the serpent with his
   heel,
> Since God is marching on."

He has sounded forth the trumpet that shall never call
   retreat;
He is sifting out the hearts of men before his
   judgement-seat:
Oh! be swift, my soul, to answer Him! Be jubilant, my
   feet!
> Our God is marching on.

In the beauty of the lilies Christ was born across the sea,
With a glory in his bosom that transfigures you and me:
As he died to make men holy, let us live to make men
   free,
> While God is marching on.

Julia Ward Howe (1819–1910)

I like to be down in Sussex for Mothering Sunday in March. In the old days everyone from all the little village churches like ours would go to their Mother Church on Mothering Sunday, which I suppose for us would mean Chichester Cathedral.

But I'm happy just to get home to our village church with Jan. I love the service. Sometimes the children bring their mothers little pots of primroses. Then they give primroses to all the other mothers, whose children aren't there, and then to anyone who hopes to be a mother one day, and then to anyone who ever had a mother . . . Yes, in the end we all get a pot of primroses, mothers, fathers, maiden aunts, everybody! Jan always plants hers out underneath the wall, and they've all grown and spread so they make quite a display in the garden now.

One Mothering Sunday Jan gave me a beautiful picture of a flower embroidered with the words:

> God couldn't be everywhere –
> That's why he created Mothers!

And I sometimes wish I could find one to give to her, which says:

> God couldn't be everywhere –
> That's why he gave us daughters!

Jan and Scotty and I have always been a very close, loving family, even though we've had a lot of separations. Perhaps it's been a case of "Absence makes the heart grow fonder"!

We lived in Morecambe during the war, but I was

working in the theatre in London, with only Sundays free. Scotty was away serving in the RAF, and, like everyone else, I never knew where he was or when we would next see him. And it wasn't always easy for me to get home to Morecambe because, as some of you will remember, there were strict wartime travelling restrictions.

After the performance on Saturday night I used to try to catch the five to eleven from Euston to Lancaster. Often the trains were so full of troops, they wouldn't allow civilians on. One night I was there and I saw a boy I knew from Morecambe among the soldiers, so I got on and chatted to him. When the fellow who collected the tickets came along I looked piteous and said, "I just came as far as London to meet my husband, home on leave" and the boy played along, so I got away with it.

I'd get off the train at Lancaster — it used to take something over six hours, so it was early morning by then — and travel the rest of the way in the big van that was taking the newspapers to Morecambe, because I knew the driver.

At 6.40 on Monday morning, I'd catch the boat train back to London.

I used to get home every three weeks to see Jan and to remind her who her mother was! Jan had a wonderful Nanny, Vera Heywood, known to us all as Ve. Ve loved Jan dearly, but never took any of Jan's love away from us: her Daddy was away winning the war, according to Ve, and her Mummy was working for the family.

Ve died recently, and our family has lost someone very dear to us. I was very proud to know her, and all my life I shall be grateful to Vera Heywood.

Jan always wanted to be an actress. When she was a little girl she called herself "Rosy Smith" and she would make entrances into our sitting room and perform her own plays. One of her plays that Scotty and I watched very often was called "Is John in?" – and that was also the entire script. Jan would go round the room knocking on imaginary doors, asking "Is John in?" – I suppose the non-speaking , invisible people who answered these doors must have said, "No, he's not", because Jan would gradually change from cheerful optimism to deep despair, and the play would end with her dying dramatically on the carpet, while the audience, Scotty and I, sat there in wonder! Our living room at our house, Prompt Corner, must have been the busiest, if the smallest, theatre in the world!

Jan later became a successful child actress, and a very professional children's television presenter at the tender age of twelve. And she grew up to be a star! Eventually she married and went to live in Beverly Hills, and although we had wonderful times when we visited her every year, we naturally saw much less of her.

For sixteen years I never let a week go by without writing to her, even if it was just a little message scribbled on the back of a page of script, to let her know how much we were thinking about her. I personally think that a loving letter is worth any number of telephone calls, don't you? Because you can reread it, and remind yourself that you are loved. Although our telephone bills would have made your hair curl, too!

Every Christmas, carol singers would come from St James', Lancaster Gate and stand below our window. We'd telephone Jan, and hold the receiver out of the window so she could hear them singing "Away in a Manger" and then they'd all shout: "Happy Christmas, Jan!"

And on New Year's Eve, just before midnight, either

we would telephone Jan, or she'd call us, and we'd hold our receiver to the television set, so that she could listen from Beverly Hills to Big Ben striking midnight in London.

God Be With You Till We Meet Again

God be with you till we meet again,
By his counsels guide, uphold you,
With his sheep securely fold you:
God be with you till we meet again.

God be with you till we meet again,
'Neath his wings protecting hide you,
Daily manna still provide you:
God be with you till we meet again.

God be with you till we meet again,
When life's perils thick confound you,
Put his arms unfailing round you:
God be with you till we meet again.

God be with you till we meet again,
Keep love's banner floating o'er you,
Smile death's threatening wave before you:
God be with you till we meet again.

Jeremiah Eames Rankin (1824–1904)

Several years ago Jan came home to England. Oh! It's lovely to have her back with us. Jan and her husband, William, live in a beautiful home in Sussex, where Scotty and I have our cottage, and **Praise Be!** is recorded each year.

And now in March, Jan, William, Scotty and I are all busy gardeners – hoeing, pruning, sowing seeds in boxes in the greenhouse, feeding the roses, mulching the camellias (Oh, yes! We're very technical – we put old tea-leaves round the bases!), weeding, and getting the garden – not to forget our London window-box – all tidy before that other mother, Mother Nature, goes mad in April!

It's a month of many holy days, March, have you noticed? On St David's Day there's always very good singing on *Songs of Praise* from Wales, and Scotty and I join in at home. Usually it's Lent all through March, with the churches bare and plain, no flowers or embroidered altar cloths, and rather solemn hymns each Sunday.

Songs of Praise goes to Ireland for St Patrick's Day, where they sing a great favourite, St Patrick's Breastplate, Mrs Alexander's translation of the old gaelic hymn ''Lorica''. Some say that St Patrick wrote it himself. One verse is rather different from all the rest. I know a lot of you like the prayerful words:

St Patrick's Breastplate

Christ be with me, Christ within me,
Christ behind me, Christ before me,
Christ beside me, Christ to win me,
Christ to comfort and restore me,
Christ beneath me, Christ above me,
Christ in quiet, Christ in danger,
Christ in hearts of all that love me,
Christ in mouth of friend and stranger.

Ascribed to St Patrick
Tr. Mrs C.F. Alexander
(1818–95)

April

It's a warm wind, the west wind, full of birds' cries;
I never hear the west wind but tears are in my eyes,
For it comes from the west lands, the old brown hills,
And April's in the west wind, and daffodils.

from The West Wind by John Masefield

I wish you could all come to Jan's April Plant Sale one
year. She holds it to help raise money for the church. All
the village seems to come along, but although we are
often filming **Praise Be!** in April, for some reason we
always manage to miss the Plant Sale. It's a shame,
because it's a wonderful "do". My job is to run a little
stall selling teas and coffees — and take it from me, no
one goes past *my* stall without buying!

Old parish churches like ours need such a lot of money
to keep them going. There always seems to be something
— dry rot in the woodwork, a leak in the roof, broken
glass or tiles. Sad to say, sometimes vandals break in and
do wanton, senseless damage, like ripping up the prayer
books or smashing beautiful ancient tombs of families
who lived and worshipped there hundreds of years ago.
What makes anyone want to do things like that?

We Christians must patiently keep putting things back
to rights. As usual, John Betjeman has the word for it.

On country mornings sharp and clear
The penitent in faith draw near
And kneeling here below
Partake the Heavenly Banquet spread
Of Sacramental Wine and Bread
And Jesus' presence know.

And must that plaintive bell in vain
Plead loud along the dripping lane?
And must the building fall?
Not while we love the Church and live
And of our charity will give
Our much, our more, our all.

Extract from *Verses Turned in Aid of
A Public Subscription* 1952 John Betjeman

In the first volume of my *Praise Be! Notebook* I wrote that
there has been one thing that I have always wanted to
do – to ride in a little cart pulled by a donkey! The ink
was hardly dry on the page before my wish came true
– as you will have seen if you watched the 1990 series
of **Praise Be!** There was Thora in her deerstalker hat,
driving a cart pulled along by a dear little donkey called
Martha, and the BBC recorded this historic moment for
posterity – and the **Praise Be!** opening title sequence!
I felt I ought to be singing that song, how does it go?
"No wheels on my wagon, but I'm still rolling
along! . . ."
What a glorious April day that was, visiting the Donkey
Sanctuary at Sidmouth. Elizabeth Svendson has spent a
lifetime rescuing and caring for ill-treated, unwanted or
worn out donkeys. Once they get to her, the donkeys are

secure and well cared for for the rest of their donkeys' years.

Elizabeth told me on **Praise Be!** about how she also travels to poorer, "third world" countries, where donkeys work hard for the families they belong to – the donkey is transport, tractor, and – well, really, the entire work force. But often in these countries the donkeys only live to be eight or nine, when they should live "donkeys' years" – thirty or more. Elizabeth teaches the owners how to give their donkeys healthier, happier, longer lives, which is good for the donkeys, but of course it's also good for the people themselves.

I met lots of donkeys that day. Do you know, there are more than 4000 living at the Sanctuary? They've had to buy a computer to record all their details. Yet every donkey receives a lot of love and individual attention, and they all have very big personalities of their own, and of course, they are all given their own names if they arrive without one. If you ever go to visit them – and they are open every day and make visitors very welcome – ask someone if you can meet my namesake. Yes! The night before we were there, one of the donkeys gave birth to a little boy, mushroom grey, like a thunder cloud, and they've named him after me – Thor!

Sometimes on *Songs of Praise* for Palm Sunday we're shown a little donkey being led along by the Sunday School children into the church or cathedral. They look so proud of themselves, with their neat little feet!

The Donkey

When fishes flew and forests walked
And figs grew upon thorn,
Some moment when the moon was blood
Then surely I was born;

With monstrous head and sickening cry
And ears like errant wings,
The devil's walking parody
On all four-footed things.

The tattered outlaw of the earth,
Of ancient crooked will;
Starve, scourge, deride me: I am dumb,
I keep my secret still.

Fools! For I also had my hour;
One far fierce hour and sweet:
There was a shout about my ears,
And palms before my feet!

G. K. Chesterton (1874–1936)

Sometimes Easter is in March, sometimes in April. Why can't it always be on the same day every year, like Christmas? I used to think the Government chose which day Easter would be on! But of course they don't – it's all to do with the full moon.

Have you ever looked at all those pages at the front of the Book of Common Prayer, before you get to the prayers? There are lots of Calendars and Tables of Lessons and Alternative Tables of Lessons. There's also "A Table to find Easter Day" – have you ever studied that? Well, I'll tell you, in this table there are three columns, the first is headed: Golden Number, the second: Day of the Month and the third: Sunday Letter. And this is what it says you have to do to find out when Easter will fall in any year:

"To find the Golden Number, or Prime, add one to the Year of our Lord, and then divide by 19; the remainder, if any, is the Golden Number; but if nothing remaineth, then 19 is the Golden Number . . ."

Now do pay attention! What do we do next?

"Look for the Golden Number of the year, against which stands the day of the Paschal Full Moon; then look in the third Column for the Sunday Letter, next after the day of the Full Moon, and the day of the Month standing against that Sunday Letter is Easter Day."

A cinch! And once you've mastered that, turn over the page and what do you find? "Another Table to Find Easter" – I think I'll leave that for someone like Paul Daniels to explain. I still haven't fathomed the first one. Learning to work a video is easier. No, all right, I can't do that either.

However you reckon it, I prefer it when Easter falls in April rather than March, don't you? I love to see the graves in the churchyard full of primroses, and bright daffodils nodding their yellow bonnets at us as we walk along the path on a warm April day.

> When the March winds do blow
> We shall have snow
> And what will the Robin do then,
> Poor thing?

Mind you, in the north it can sometimes still be snowing even in April. I remember one April we were filming interviews for **Praise Be!**, and I'd gone to meet Geoffrey Smith in his garden in Yorkshire. It was to be a story for Easter about new life returning to the earth every Spring, with a few helpful hints for us gardeners, from an expert, thrown in!

It was a cold and frosty Spring morning in Harrogate when I set out with the film crew to find Geoffrey's lovely old stone farm house high in the Yorkshire moors. When Geoffrey and I were having a cup of coffee and getting to know one another, he suddenly said, "Oh look!" A graceful snowflake was floating down outside the window, followed by several million others! Before we could even begin our interview, his garden disappeared in the snow!

But that's show business. Fortunately Geoffrey had lots of pansies and things with Latin names in pots in his greenhouse, and we soon created an indoor garden in his sitting room. Daffodils bring their own sunshine into a room. Set in a big bowl by the window, with the snow falling outside, they were as good as a garden the size of a park for showing the triumph of faith, hope and love over death and defeat. So Geoffrey and I were able to have a very happy chat about gardens and glory and God.

The Day of Resurrection

The Day of Resurrection:
Earth, tell it out abroad;
The Passover of gladness,
The Passover of God!
From death to life eternal,
From earth unto the sky,
Our Christ hath brought us over
With hymns of victory.

Our hearts be pure from evil,
That we may see aright
The Lord in rays eternal
Of resurrection-light;
And, listening to his accents,
May hear so calm and plain
His own "All hail", and, hearing,
May raise the victor strain.

Now let the heavens be joyful,
And earth her song begin,
The round world keep high triumph,
And all that is therein;
Let all things seen and unseen
Their notes of gladness blend,
For Christ the Lord hath risen,
Our Joy that hath no end.

St John Damascene 750
trs. J. M. Neale

May

All shall be well, and all shall be well and all manner of things shall be well.

From Revelations of Divine Love
by St Julian of Norwich (1343–1443), whose day is 8 May

Soon after Scotty and I were married on 3 May, the minister from one of our local churches asked me if I would do some work for him. He had boxes full of bits of paper, which were the records of the deaths of all the people who had been to his church from the 18th century. He wanted me to sort out all their names, when they died, and where they were interred, and then write it out on beautiful parchment paper in a book, for displaying in the church, a different page being shown each week of the year. It was so everyone could be remembered, not just the ones who could afford a coloured glass window or memorial plaque.

I think I got the job because I had nice handwriting. It took weeks and weeks, sorting out those boxes. I had to ask Scotty to help me. I learnt a lot from doing it. For instance, it's rather sad this, but so often if a wife died, a few weeks later her husband would die, and vice versa.

I got a book out from the library to study the old English writing, and I bought myself a proper mapping pen. And all this work for the princely sum of four guineas! But even at the time, I remember thinking: "This will be here long after I'm gone."

I wonder if it is! If you ever go there, you could ask to look at the old records. Well, so could I! Do you think you'll still be able to see Thora's handiwork, up to the year 1937 anyway – or have they transferred it all to a dreaded Word Processor?

A few years ago Scotty and I celebrated our Golden Wedding – and it still don't seem a day too much! Oh, but you should have seen him when I first met him. He was so handsome, and always dressed in the very latest fashions!

As I've had to confess before on **Praise Be!**, because people often ask, neither Scotty nor I can remember what hymns we sang on our wedding day. But when I tell you that we processed out of the chapel by the wrong door, while all our friends and the photographer on his ladder were waiting outside another door, you can see what sort of a state we were in!

The hymn I would choose today, if we were to do it all over again – which I gladly would – would be "O Perfect Love".

O Perfect Love

O perfect Love, all human thought transcending,
Lowly we kneel in prayer before your throne,
That theirs may be the love which knows no ending,
Whom you for evermore now join as one.

O perfect Life, be now their full assurance
Of tender charity and steadfast faith,
Of patient hope, and quiet, brave endurance,
With childlike trust that fears nor pain nor death.

Grant them the joy which brightens earthly sorrow,
Grant them the peace which calms all earthly strife;
And to life's day the glorious unknown morrow
That dawns upon eternal love and life.

Dorothy Frances Gurney (1858–1932)

May is a busy month on **Praise Be!** We're usually still recording the last programmes, while watching the first ones begin to go out on the air each Sunday. A lot of the letters that come in now mention how much you enjoy seeing Jan's Muscovy ducks, who always seem to be following me about when I go into the garden. A kind lady called Joyce, from the Scilly Isles, sent me this little poem about ducks – but unfortunately I haven't been able to trace who originally wrote it:

When God had finished the stars and whirl of coloured
    suns
He turned His mind from big things, to fashion little ones.

Beautiful, tiny things (like daisies) He made, and then
He made the comical ones in case the minds of men
Should stiffen and become
Dull, humourless and glum,
And so forgetful of their Maker be
As to take even themselves *quite seriously*!

Caterpillars and cats are lively and excellent puns,
All God's jokes are good – even the practical ones.
And as for the duck, I think God must have smiled a bit
Seeing those bright eyes blink on the day He fashioned it.
And He's probably laughing still
At the sound that came out of its bill!

Anon

I've always loved the month of May – my birthday
month. Scotty, who is as good-looking as ever, well I
think so, has already had his eightieth birthday, but the
funny thing is, neither of us feel any different from when
we were young and twenty. Well – not much different!

The only thing you have to remember, as you get older,
is to pace yourself. Scotty and I have both begun to learn
this. There's a huge modern shopping precinct,
Whiteleys, not far from where we live. We enjoy strolling
along and having a good look round. One day we had
spent quite a long time there, and we realized that we
were both ready for home. As we got outside onto the
pavement, two walking sticks went smartly up into the
air and we both called out in unison: "Taxi!"

Taxi? We were only five minutes walk away from home!

We haven't stopped doing any of the things we enjoy
(if I ever do feel old, it's when I've got nothing to do)
but we just go at a gentler pace. And I've discovered that
there's a lot more to be enjoyed in life when you do slow
yourself down. Well, as the writer of this modern version
of the 23rd Psalm puts it:

The Lord is my Pace-setter – I shall not rush.

He makes me stop for quiet intervals,

He provides me with images of stillness which restore my serenity,

He leads me in ways of efficiency through calmness of mind,

And his guidance is peace.

Even though I have a great many things to accomplish each day,

I will not fret,

For his Presence is here,

His timelessness, His all-importance, will keep me in balance.

He prepares refreshment and renewal in the midst of my activity,

By anointing my mind with His oils of tranquillity,

My cup of joyous energy overflows.

Truly harmony and effectiveness shall be the fruits of my hours,

For I shall walk at the pace of my Lord

And dwell in His house for ever.

May is the Church's birthday, too, on Whitsunday. Well, some people call it Pentecost, because it comes on the 50th day after Easter, but I've always known it as Whitsunday. When we were young there used to be the famous Whitsunday processions in Manchester, with all the denominations joining in, and the Sunday School children dressed in white. I wonder, do they still do that anywhere? I haven't seen one for years.

It's the time in the New Testament, after Jesus had risen from the dead and ascended into heaven, when the Holy

Ghost appeared to descend on the disciples in tongues of flame. Everyone was – understandably – amazed! They were ordinary men one moment, the next they were Apostles, who knew just what they had to do and say to tell all the world about Jesus. So that was the beginning of the Church, the same one that you and I go to today. And that's why Whitsunday is the Church's birthday.

It's a happy, festive season, and we sing the hymns I like best – the cheerful ones with lots of Allelujahs in them. Scotty and I often sing the chorus of this next one in two parts, when we're working about the house or garden – we're getting so good at it, we should go professional!

O Happy Day!

O happy day! that fixed my choice
On Thee, my Saviour and my God!
Well may this glowing heart rejoice,
And tell its raptures all abroad.

O happy day! O happy Day!
When Jesus washed my sins away;
He taught me how to watch and pray,
And live rejoicing every day (Hallelujah!)
Happy day! O happy day!
When Jesus washed my sins away.

'Tis done, the great transaction's done!
I am my Lord's, and He is mine!
He drew me, and I followed on,
Charmed to confess the voice divine.

O happy day! O happy day!
When Jesus washed my sins away;
He taught me how to watch and pray,
And live rejoicing every day (Hallelujah!)
Happy day! O happy day!
When Jesus washed my sins away.

Ron Jones *(Mission Praise)*

Summer

My Garden

A garden is a lovesome thing, God wot!
Rose plot,
Fringed pool,
Ferned grot –
The veriest school
Of peace; and yet the fool
Contends that God is not –
Not God! in gardens! when the eve is cool?
Nay, but I have a sign:
'Tis very sure God walks in mine.

T. E. Brown (1830–97)

June

> The rainbow comes and goes,
> And lovely is the rose
>
> Wordsworth

The place I most like to be on a June day is in an English garden full of old roses. Some roses will go on flowering all through the summer, but many of our most beautiful old roses flower once, in June. It's a sight I prefer not to miss.

Naturally our garden is full of that famous floribunda: Thora Hird! Or Thorabunda, as Jan calls it. Thorabunda goes on flowering all summer, being a modern rose, but it looks old-fashioned. I'm very fond of its delicate, peachy pink flowers, and they have a lovely scent. I like to have a big vaseful arranged in our sitting room all through the summer, so the whole cottage smells of roses. Some modern roses don't carry any scent, but my namesake does. (Swank! Swank!)

Sometimes I talk to my guests on **Praise Be!** at home, rather than travelling to see them, and when a dear friend, the Reverend Dr John Tudor, from the Methodist Central Hall, Westminster, came down to see me one sunny June day, we sat outside in the garden among the roses, with our cups of tea, and recalled a Christmas *Songs of Praise* which John had been involved with, linking carol-singers in Trafalgar Square with islanders on the Pacific island of Tonga. They all sang together , the Londoners in Trafalgar Square wrapped up in scarves and mufflers, the islanders on Tonga with garlands of tropical flowers round their necks. Methodist missionaries had first taken Christianity to Tonga, so as well as all the traditional carols, they sang the lively mission carol: "Go, tell it on the mountain."

Go Tell It On The Mountain

Go, tell it on the mountain
Over the hills and everywhere;
Go, tell it on the mountain
That Jesus Christ is born.

While shepherds sat a-watching
Their silent flocks by night,
There shone throughout the heavens
A great and glorious light.

The shepherds feared and trembled
When, high above the earth,
Rang out the angel chorus
That hailed our Saviour's birth.

Go, tell it on the mountain,
Over the hills and everywhere;
Go, tell it on the mountain
That Jesus Christ is born!

American Traditional

Meg Merrilies

Old Meg she was a Gipsy
And lived upon the Moors:
Her bed it was the brown heath turf,
And her house was out of doors.

Her apples were swart blackberries,
Her currants pods o' broom;
Her wine was dew of the wild white rose,
Her book a churchyard tomb.

Her brothers were the craggy hills,
Her sisters larchen trees –
Alone with her great family
She lived as she did please.

No breakfast had she many a morn,
No dinner many a noon,
And 'stead of supper she would stare
Full hard against the moon.

But every morn of woodbine fresh
She made her garlanding,
And every night the dark glen yew
She wove, and she would sing.

And with her fingers, old and brown
She plaited mats o' rushes,
And she gave them to the cottagers
She met among the bushes.

> Old Meg was brave as Margaret Queen,
> And tall as Amazon;
> An old red blanket cloak she wore,
> A chip hat had she on.
> God rest her aged bones somewhere,
> She died full long agone.
>
> John Keats

Oh! Meg Merrilies. That was one of my favourite songs that we all used to sing at school, and I can still recite almost all of it by heart.

Does anyone remember, before the war, listening to wireless programmes with "Romany"? He used to be on Children's Hour. His grandfather was a gipsy, Cornelius Smith, a wild drinking man and a vagabond, who one day was converted to Christianity, and, because this was the way with gipsy families, his whole family was converted too.

Romany's real name was George Bramwell Evans. His mother was Cornelius Smith's youngest daughter, Tilly, and his father was a Salvation Army officer. Young Bramwell Evans became a Wesleyan Methodist Minister, but he never lost his old ancestral gipsy love of the natural world.

In his broadcasts, as "Romany", he took his young listeners on spellbinding walks through the countryside, telling them about the flowers and trees in the woodland, the birds and insects and little mammals, and all the things he could see. But he never left the studio! It was all done with the magic of words, Romany's wonderful descriptive skills making you feel you could almost see the things he was talking about. I've sometimes heard people say that they prefer radio to television because "the pictures are better"!

For anyone who was a child then, this poem, written as a farewell to Romany after his death in 1943 by another Children's Hour broadcaster, Geoffrey Dearmer, may bring back some fond memories:

Farewell To Romany

Goodbye, dear friend. If we no more shall roam
Fresh woods with you, nor fields your voice made cool;
Nor find the fieldmouse in his harvest home,
The brown trout in the pool;

Nor with hands made more gentle at your words,
Pick up the shrew mouse or the trembling hare;
Nor, with ears wiser, name the singing birds
In trees no longer bare.

If we no more with you shall do these things,
Let us, at least, say sometimes when the clear
Spring skies are full of song and woods with wings,
"I wish that he was here."

Then shall we keep your memory green and true:
Then shall the lovely world more lovely grow,
And you, dear Romany, I think that you
Would wish to have it so.

Geoffrey Dearmer

I'm quite nomadic myself, when I'm working on **Praise Be!** We go all over the country tracking down places where hymns were inspired or written, and meeting Christians from all walks of life.

Whenever we go down to the West Country, we drive along the A303, and pass near Stonehenge, that ancient circle of enormous stones, older than the Roman occupation. You can see it up on the hillside above you as you drive along, and I'm always fascinated by it. It doesn't seem to matter what time of year, there are always people there, standing and staring; and especially in June, because some people believe that Stonehenge was built round a Druid sun-worshipping ceremony, held at sunrise on the longest day of the year, 21 June. People are kept well away from the stones themselves and walk round and round the perimeter fence, like moths to the flame of a mystery.

I realize ancient sites like Stonehenge have to be protected. Of course they do. But I sometimes think our beautiful cathedrals are over-protected. They also receive hundreds of visitors each day, many of them in search of something, they don't know what. There may not be a perimeter fence round the outside, but areas inside are often dark and cordoned off, unexplained no-go areas, and sometimes the only really welcoming place is the Cathedral shop. Our ancient cathedrals and churches are very beautiful, mysterious places but as long as visitors come up against perimeter fences, real or imagined, don't you think they might walk round and round for ever, without getting a glimpse of the loving God that inspired them?

O Thou Not Made With Hands

O thou not made with hands,
Not throned above the skies,
Nor walled with shining walls,
Nor framed with stones of price,
More bright than gold or gem,
God's own Jerusalem!

Where'er the gentle heart
Finds courage from above;
Where'er the heart forsook
Warms with the breath of love;
Where faith bids fear depart,
City of God, thou art.

Thou art where'er the proud
In humbleness melts down;
Where self itself yields up;
Where martyrs win their crown;
Where faithful souls possess
Themselves in perfect peace.

Where in life's common ways
With cheerful feet we go;
Where in his steps we tread,
Who trod the way of woe;
Where he is in the heart,
City of God, thou art.

Not throned above the skies,
Nor golden-walled afar,
But where Christ's two or three

In his name gathered are,
Be in the midst of them,
God's own Jerusalem.

F. T. Palgrave (1824–97)

For children at school, June is the month when they have to face all their important examinations. The days are at their longest, and it stays light very late, so even after "lights out" many a June night is spent by anxious youngsters trying to cram into their brains all those dates and names, facts and figures that they've been yawning over and paying too little attention to all year!

I was never much of a clever-head myself, at school, except at arithmetic. I've always had a very good head for figures, and I can still add up my shopping bill faster than most shop assistants, even with their calculators.

And they were happy days, my schooldays. I know I've told you before how I left school when I was fourteen, and on the first day of the next term, while my old classmates were walking back to school along the road outside, I stood at home sadly looking out of the window, dressed in my school uniform. What a pathetic sight! My dear mother came in and, instead of teasing me, she said, "Get your satchel and run along and see if Miss Nelson will have you back for another term." And I flew!

On Trinity Sunday each June, I'm reminded of that day, because we sang Holy, Holy, Holy! at school assembly for the first day of the new term, and the loudest voice of all was Thora's!

Holy, Holy, Holy!

Holy, holy, holy! Lord God almighty!
Early in the morning our song shall rise to thee;
Holy, holy, holy! merciful and mighty!
God in three Persons, blessèd Trinity!

Holy, holy, holy! all the saints above thee,
Casting down their golden crowns around the glassy sea;
Cherubim and seraphim falling down before thee,
Which wert, and art, and evermore shall be.

Holy, holy, holy! though the darkness hide thee,
Though the eye of sinful man thy glory may not see,
Only thou art holy, there is none beside thee
Perfected in power, in love, and purity.

Holy, holy, holy! Lord God almighty!
All thy works shall praise thy name in earth,
    and sky, and sea;
Holy, holy, holy! merciful and mighty!
God in three persons, blessèd Trinity!

                                        Bishop R. Heber (1733–1826)

One afternoon early in June, I was out in the garden
weeding one of the beds, and I heard Jan's car crunching
on the gravel. She called over to me, "Can you come here
a minute – just for a tick?" I didn't ask what she wanted,
I went over, and she said, "Come with me. It won't take
a minute." So I got in the car and off we went, out of
the gate, left into the lane, and then for about another

couple of miles. We stopped by a gate leading into a wood.

We got out and there was no need for her to explain anything. The entire floor of the wood was the deepest, richest blue you ever saw. There didn't look as though there would have been room for one more bluebell. Blueness just bounced upwards through the trees. I shall remember it as long as I live.

When we got home, I went back to my weeding, and I thought, "What a funny family we are!"

The following year we wanted to go back at the same time with the **Praise Be!** film crew, to share the scene with the viewers, but that year the bluebells had come much earlier, and were almost over when we arrived. I think there's probably only one day a year, perhaps even only one hour, when the bluebells are perfect, and I'm very grateful to Jan for taking me there at the exact moment.

As we drove home Jan and I were singing – no prizes for guessing – All things bright and beautiful! And it's never been more heartfelt!

All Things Bright and Beautiful

All things bright and beautiful,
All creatures great and small,
All things wise and wonderful,
The Lord God made them all.

Each little flower that opens,
Each little bird that sings,
He made their golden colours,
He made their tiny wings.

The purple-headed mountain,
The river running by,
The sunset, and the morning
That brightens up the sky:

The cold wind in the winter,
The pleasant summer sun,
The ripe fruits in the garden,
He made them, every one.

The tall trees in the greenwood,
The meadows where we play,
The rushes by the water
We gather every day:

He gave us eyes to see them,
And lips that we might tell
How great is God Almighty,
Who has made all things well.

All things bright and beautiful,
All creatures great and small,
All things wise and wonderful,
The Lord God made them all.

                    Mrs C. F. Alexander (1818–95)

Praise Be! usually comes to an end in June, and Scotty
and I feel quite sad as we watch the last programme going
out. Like the old roses when they start to fade at the end
of June, it always seems to be over too soon. I must admit,
I sometimes feel a bit flat.

That's why, when our postman calls the next day with

more of your letters, it means so much to me. They cheer me up and reminnd me that I've made some good friends among all the millions of people who watch *Songs of Praise* and **Praise Be!** and love the hymns as much as I do. And there's always next year to look forward to . . . D.V.!

July

> "Joy is the flag on the citadel of the heart,
> when the King is in residence"

One great joy for me has been joining the cast of *Last of the Summer Wine*. Scotty and I have laughed so much watching the series for years, long before I knew I would be a little part of it. A while back on **Praise Be!** not very long before he died so suddenly and unexpectedly, I interviewed Joe Gladwyn, a good Christian, and a dear friend, who you'll remember used to play Norah Batty's husband, Wally Batty. But I didn't know even then that I'd soon be joining the cast.

A lot of the comedy is done with gestures and expression rather than dialogue. Sometimes my script arrives with hardly any words on it at all, and I wonder what I can possibly make of it. But my family nickname isn't "Face" for nothing. If I've nothing to say, I can *look* volumes!

My character, Edie, knows as much about driving a car as I do — nothing! So I especially enjoyed doing the episode when she was having a driving lesson from her husband, Wesley, and she said, "Have you moved the gears? They were over the other side yesterday!" I'm sure I'd be just the same if Scotty was ever rash enough to try to teach me how to drive!

Last of the Summer Wine shows a happy picture of a simpler world, of people going through life just being themselves. And modern technology — from pop-up toasters to washing machines – far from being glamorous status symbols, always seems to be making idiots out of the human beings.

It's always the same basic plot: three old men, one a clever-clogs, the other two irresponsible and carefree, shamble around their home town, innocently causing havoc wherever they go, while a group of stern northern women, like women since time immemorial, sit in judgement on them!

Most of the comedy series I've been in over recent years have been set in the north of England, so I've been able to spend many happy summers in a part of the world and among the people I know and love so well. It's yet another blessing I'm always thanking "Him Upstairs" for.

Yes, God is Good

Yes, God is good – in earth and sky,
From ocean depths and spreading wood,
Ten thousand voices seem to cry:
God made us all, and God is good.

The sun that keeps his trackless way,
And downward pours his golden flood,
Night's sparkling hosts, all seem to say
In accents clear, that God is good.

The joyful birds prolong the strain,
Their song with every spring renewed;
The air we breathe, and falling rain,
Each softly whispers: God is good.

I hear it in the rushing breeze;
The hills that have for ages stood,
The echoing sky and roaring seas,
All swell the chorus: God is good.

Yes, God is good, all nature says,
By God's own hand with speech endued;
And man, in louder notes of praise,
Should sing for joy that God is good.

For all your gifts we bless you, Lord,
But chiefly for our heavenly food;
Your pardoning grace, your quickening word,
These prompt our song, that God is good.

John Hampden Gurney (1802–62)

July 15 is St Swithin's Day, and Scotty and I always peer
anxiously out of the window first thing in the morning
to see if it looks like rain. You know the old proverb:

St Swithin's Day, if thou dost rain,
For forty days it will remain:
St Swithin's Day, if thou be fair,
For forty days 'twill rain na mair.

I love all those old weather sayings, don't you? As long
as you take them with a good pinch of salt. Every village
seems to have its own amateur weather men, with their
own local lore: ''Oo ar! if the wind be in the east, and
the moon on the wane, every day 'til Candlemas, be sure
'twill rain!'' or ''If in the morning you see St Mildred's

steeple, there'll be a gale by afternoon, a-blowing all the people.'' I don't know where they get them from! They look up at the sky, and predict all sorts of gloom and doom for the neighbourhood.

These days everyone's talking about ''global warming'' and ''the greenhouse effect'', and those old weather prophets have got nothing on the doom and gloom that's being forecast by the newspapers.

I believe, as I always have, that everything is in the good Lord's hands. He'll look after this old world, and show us what to do. I think it's far more important to wonder how Christian and caring we are being, than how ''green'' we are – whatever that means.

Jesus talked about proverbs and the signs that tell us about nature, and they were just the same in his day as they are now:

''When evening comes, you say, 'It will be fair weather, for the sky is red,' and in the morning, 'Today it will be stormy, for the sky is red and overcast.' ''

St Matthew 16:2–3(NIV)

But he also spoke of looking deeper, for more important signs of the times:

He said to the crowd:

''When you see a cloud rising in the west, immediately you say, 'It's going to rain', and it does. And when the south wind blows, you say, 'It's going to be hot', and it is.

''Hypocrites! You know how to interpret the

appearance of the earth and the sky. How is it that you
don't know how to interpret this present time?

"Why don't you judge for yourselves what is right?"

St Luke 12:54–7 (NIV)

Judge Eternal

Judge eternal, throned in splendour,
Lord of lords and King of kings,
With thy living fire of judgement
Purge this realm of bitter things:
Solace all its wide dominion
With the healing of thy wings.

Still the weary folk are pining
For the hour that brings release:
And the city's crowded clangour
Cries aloud for sin to cease;
And the homesteads and the woodlands
Plead in silence for their peace.

Crown, O God, thine own endeavour:
Cleave our darkness with thy sword:
Feed the faint and hungry heathen
With the richness of thy Word:
Cleanse the body of this empire
Through the glory of the Lord.

Henry Scott Holland (1847–1916)

A week after St Swithin's Day, comes St Mary Magdalene's Day, on 22 July. Mary Magdalene had a bad reputation as a loose woman when she first met Jesus, but of all his followers, she had the warmest, most human love for him. So there's hope for all of us, however badly we may think we've behaved. Like Mary, Jesus' mother, Mary Magdalene stood by the Cross to the bitter end; and she rose before dawn, the first person to visit his tomb on Easter morning.

One Easter morning Jan and I got up before dawn and went to church for the Easter Vigil. There was a fire of twigs outside the church, and we all stood round it, singing hymns, until the sun began to rise. Then we were quiet, and for a few moments there was absolute silence.

Just as the sun appeared over the horizon, all at once and all together, the birds began to sing. I think every bird in Sussex must have come along to our church that morning. You never heard such a sound: thrushes, sparrows, robins, starlings, larks, blue-tits, all singing their heads off – but loudest of all were the blackbirds.

The Blackbird

Magdalen at Michael's gate
Tirled at the pin.
On Joseph's thorn sang the blackbird,
"Let her in, let her in."

"See-est thou the wounds?" said Michael.
"Knowest thou the sin?"
"She is sorry, sorry, sorry," sang the blackbird,
"Let her in, let her in."

"Yes, I have seen the wounds
And I know my sin."
"She knows it well, well, well," sang the blackbird,
"Let her in, let her in."

"Thou bringest no offering;", said Michael.
"Nought save sin."
And the blackbird sang, "She is sorry, sorry, sorry,
Let her in, let her in."

When he had sung himself to sleep
And night did begin,
One came out and opened Michael's gate
And Magdalen went in.

                                        Henry Kingsley

As the bees buzz outside my window on a July Sunday
afternoon, you'll sometimes find me, another busy bee,
sitting down at my desk to answer all the kind letters I've
received from people who have asked me to open their
church fetes that year. I'm sincerely sorry to tell you that
it's very rare that I can say yes. I have to be away filming
for so much of the summer, you know, or in a studio,
or rehearsing, or about a billion other things.

But I can dream, can't I? I do so love a good old-
fashioned vicarage garden party. As I chew on my pen,
I imagine what I'm missing: croquet on the lawn; Scottish
dancing by a group of little girls in kilts and very clean,
white frilly blouses, with solemn little faces, and their
Mums hovering anxiously at the front, so no one else can
see properly!

Then there'll be a gymnastic vaulting display by the

cubs and scouts; a Mother's Union home-made cake stall – sold out almost before I've cut the tape and declared the fete open! – a rifle range run by a group of sallow young men in jeans and T-shirts with alarming messages written on them, and admiring little boys hanging about nearby, with longing faces and no more pocket money; a sad looking pig, which, if you're not very careful, you may have to take home with you – when you bowl the highest score! Tables groaning with jam-jars of home-made jams and pickles; a tombola; a white elephant; jumble; a coconut shy; and best of all, the tea tent!

And me in my best hat pictured in the local newspaper over the caption "Miss Thora Hird sharing a joke with the Reverend Roger Rural Dean"!

Oh, if only!

Shall We Gather at the River?

Shall we gather at the river,
Where bright angel feet have trod,
With its crystal tide for ever
Flowing by the throne of God?

Yes, we'll gather at the river,
The beautiful, the beautiful river:
Gather with the saints at the river,
That flows by the throne of God.

On the margin of the river
Dashing up its silver spray,
We will walk and worship ever
All the happy, golden day.

Ere we reach the shining river,
Lay we every burden down;
Grace our spirits will deliver,
And provide a robe and crown.

At the shining of the river,
Mirror of the saviour's face,
Saints whom death will never sever
Raise their song of saving grace.

Soon we'll reach the silver river,
Soon our pilgrimage will cease;
Soon our happy hearts will quiver
With the melody of peace.

Yes, we'll gather at the river,
The beautiful, the beautiful river:
Gather with the saints at the river,
That flows by the throne of God.

Everything's so bright and abundant and colourful in
July. I walk round the garden at home, and I keep saying
to Scotty, "Look at those! Look! Look! Look there!" And
it's all come out of the bare earth, and just a few packets
of seeds!

Do you know what it reminds me of? The post-war
years, and the very first Technicolor films that we ever
saw . . . Honestly! We could hardly believe our eyes.
We'd all got so used to wearing drab clothes, and
everything looking dull and dreary. I think those brightly
coloured films brought happiness and hope to an entire
generation who had just come through the long grey

years of war. Of course, I did get a little more blasé once Jan and I both started appearing in some of them!

Now the wheel has turned full circle, and many "arty" directors are making their films in black and white again. It's a funny old world. At least we know the flowers won't start coming up in black and white one July!

If your church is called either St Thomas's or St James's, you'll have your patronal festival in July, and I bet your flower arrangers really go to town that Sunday. It's a good month for visiting churches, whatever their Saint's name, if you've got a free day, because so many of them hold July Flower Festivals.

While the Bishops and other leaders of the Church are meeting in solemn assembly in York, to decide weighty matters at the July General Synod, life in the parish churches centres round urgent questions about whether or not an arrangement of lilies entitled "Snow White and the Seven Dwarfs" is taking up too much space near the altar!

Easter comes in the Spring, but signs of resurrection are around us all through the year, and nothing seems to point to it more vividly than the changing colours of the wheat and corn fields, that in July have turned to gold.

Now the Green Blade Riseth

Now the green blade riseth from the buried grain,
Wheat that in dark earth many days has lain;
Love lives again, that with the dead has been:
Love is come again,
Like wheat that springeth green.

In the grave they laid him,
Love whom men had slain,
Thinking that never he would wake again,
Laid in the earth like grain that sleeps unseen:
Love is come again,
Like wheat that springeth green.

Forth he came at Easter, like the risen grain,
He that for three days in the grave had lain,
Quick from the dead my risen Lord is seen:
Love is come again,
Like wheat that springeth green.

When our hearts are wintry, grieving, or in pain,
Thy touch can call us back to life again,
Fields of our hearts that dead and bare have been:
Love is come again,
Like wheat that springeth green.

J. M. C. Crum (1872–1946)

August

Psalm 107

They that go down to the sea in ships, that do business
   in great waters;
These see the works of the Lord, and his wonders in the
   deep.
For he commandeth and raiseth the stormy wind, which
   lifteth up the waves thereof.
They mount up to the heaven, they go down again to
   the depths: their soul is melted because of trouble.
They reel to and fro, and stagger like a drunken man,
   and are at their wits' end.
Then they cry out unto the Lord in their trouble, and he
   bringeth them out of their distresses.
He maketh the storm a calm, so that the waves thereof
   are still.
Then are they glad because they be quiet; so he bringeth
   them unto their desired haven.

Psalm 107:23–30 (AV)

The sea has always been important to me. It is to most
of us, being an island race, but feelings about it run very
deep if you grow up beside it as we did. My Mother's
father and brothers were all fishermen, and whatever you
were doing, you always had it, you know, in the back
of your mind: what's the sea doing today?

Anyone living in a seaside town or village says goodbye to their friends and neighbours when August approaches. Not because they are going away or anything. No, no. It's because you're all going to disappear among a sea of visitors! When the local population changes from 2000 to 20,000 almost overnight, you might not run into anyone you know for weeks!

Where would the theatrical profession be without this tradition of the August family holiday by the sea? Punch and Judy men, brass bands, summer repertory theatres, variety shows, end of the pier entertainers, and all the singers and comics who started their careers as Redcoats at seaside holiday camps like Butlin's and Pontin's – they are all part of what makes up a proper English family holiday by the sea.

And what would all the old-time music hall comedians have done without that great comic personage: the seaside landlady? I don't know whether they were always funny people, or whether nature followed art, and they became funny because of all the jokes that were told about them! But who hasn't stood out in the pouring rain wondering what to do, or sat in a bus-shelter to eat their fish and chips, because they were too frightened of their landlady to go back before six?

Seaside landlady jokes have continued from Victorian vaudeville to Faulty Towers. Every actor is sure to have a fund of funny stories about them, particularly, that awesome person, the ''theatrical landlady''. There's a famous story of an actor who had digs where he had to provide his own food. One day he managed, at great expense and as a very rare treat, to buy some asparagus. He left a chop and the asparagus in the kitchen for his landlady to cook for his supper when he got home from the theatre.

That night he was really looking forward to his meal, but when it arrived there was just the chop, but no asparagus. His landlady said, "Here's your chop, darling, and I've put your bluebells in water for you!"

For the last few years *Songs of Praise* has followed in the theatrical tradition, returning each August with a season of open-air, "Seaside specials". It can be blowing a gale force 9 wind, and pouring with rain, but the good old British button up their macintoshes, up go the umbrellas, and they keep right on singing hymns like this one!

Summer Suns are Glowing

Summer suns are glowing
Over land and sea;
Happy light is flowing,
Bountiful and free.
Everything rejoices
In the mellow rays;
All earth's thousand voices
Swell the psalm of praise.

God's free mercy streameth
Over all the world,
And His banner gleameth,
Everywhere unfurled.
Broad and deep and glorious,
As the heaven above,
Shines in might victorious
His eternal love.

Lord, upon our blindness
Thy pure radiance pour;
For Thy loving-kindness
Make us love Thee more.
And, when clouds are drifting
Dark across our sky,
Then, the veil uplifting,
Father, be Thou nigh.

We will never doubt Thee
Though Thou veil Thy light;
Life is dark without Thee;
Death with Thee is bright.
Light of light, shine o'er us
On our pilgrim way;
Go Thou still before us,
To the endless day.

William Walsham How (1823–97)

It's a funny thing, how many people decide to move to the seaside when they retire. I've often wondered about it, why they would want to leave their old familiar neighbourhoods where they are known and belong to the community, to spend their last years among strangers, in a bungalow, or in a Home, by the sea.

Sometimes it turns out to be a mistake, and you find all too many lonely old people, far from H.A.P.P.Y., and bitterly regretting that they ever came to live in a seaside resort. But others seem to find the peace they are looking for, and you see them enjoying the sea air, going for their daily "constitutionals" along the promenade, happy with their own thoughts and memories for company.

When you're busy, you probably only look up at the sky or out to sea to find out what the weather is going to do. But the sky and sea are the closest we can get to picturing what eternity looks like. They are rather like huge doorways to the next world. Is it empty, or are our loved ones out there somewhere, waiting for us?

As they get older, many people choose to live near the sea so that they can look at it and wonder, and when their time comes, walking into eternity won't seem such a big step.

O Lord, you have made us very small, and we bring our years to an end like a tale that is told; help us to remember that beyond our brief day is the eternity of your love.

Reinhold Niebuhr (1892–1971)

For the best picture of the Father
Don't have your back to the Son.

Wayside Pulpit

On the 6th of August is the Feast of the Transfiguration. This is St Mark's account of what happened:

After six days Jesus took Peter, James and John with him and led them up to a high mountain, where they were all alone. There he was transfigured before them. His clothes became dazzling white, whiter than anyone in the world could bleach them.

And there appeared before them Elijah and Moses, who were talking with Jesus.

Peter said to Jesus, "Rabbi, it is good for us to be here. Let us put up three shelters – one for you, one for Moses and one for Elijah." (He did not know what to say, they were so frightened.)

Then a cloud appeared and enveloped them, and a voice came from the cloud: "This is my Son, whom I love. Listen to him!"

Suddenly, when they looked round, they no longer saw anyone with them except Jesus.

St Mark 9:2–8 (NIV)

It's just a bit difficult to understand that reading, don't you think? But I think it's a bit like the way a clever photographer can make a face you had always thought of as homely or plain appear radiantly beautiful with light. Light can also transfigure your washing up water. One minute you are grumbling to yourself as you put a pile of greasy dishes into the sink and turn on the taps. The next thing you know, the sun shines through the kitchen window, and you're looking at a basin full of rainbows. Lifting the gleaming cups and plates you've washed up out of the soapy water becomes a real pleasure - well, almost!.

The light doesn't change what it falls on. It shows the beauty that was always there. But once you have seen it, you can always see it, long after the chance sunbeam and the clever photographers have gone.

The angels keep their ancient places;
Turn but a stone, and start a wing!
'Tis ye, 'tis your estranged faces,
That miss the many-splendoured thing.

from *The Kingdom of God* by
Francis Thompson

Millions of people watch and enjoy *Songs of Praise* and
Praise Be! and I get letters from all ages and from all sorts
of backgrounds. I usually get a number of letters from
people for whom hymns are a special comfort and joy,
because they are old and ill. These are the letters that
move me very much, because the people who send them
are often so patient, brave and uncomplaining.

This prayer was sent to me by Clemency Greatorex
from Goudhurst, and I think a lot of people will share
her sentiment.

Litany for the Semi-invalid

From the fear of getting worse
    Good Lord, deliver us:
From self-pity and the temptation to play for sympathy
    Good Lord, deliver us;
From the fear that others may think we are making a fuss
    Good Lord, deliver us;
From self-conscious pride in fighting bravely against
        illness
    Good Lord, deliver us;
From refusal to accept help kindly offered
    Good Lord, deliver us.

When we are enclosed in trouble, and cannot look
    outwards
  Dear Lord, be with us.

For the time to think, because we cannot escape into
        doing
For the opportunity to listen to the problems of others
For the kindness and wisdom of those who help us
For the understanding and skill of doctors and nurses
For the work of those researching new medicines and
    ways of healing
  We praise you, Good Lord.

In the name of God the Father, whose strength is ever
    with us
And of God the Son, whose suffering delivered us
And of God the Holy Ghost, whose presence is our
    constant comfort. Amen.

The long hot days of August can be quite a trial for
anyone who isn't well. There was a great response when
one evening I included this next hymn on **Praise Be!**:

At Even, Ere The Sun Was Set

At even, ere the sun was set,
The sick, O Lord, around thee lay;
O in what divers pains they met!
O with what joy they went away!

Once more 'tis eventide, and we
Oppressed with various ills draw near;
What if thy form we cannot see?
We know and feel that thou art here.

O Saviour Christ, our woes dispel;
For some are sick, and some are sad,
And some have never loved thee well,
And some have lost the love they had;

And some have found the world is vain,
Yet from the world they break not free;
And some have friends who give them pain,
Yet have not sought a friend in thee;

And none, O Lord, have perfect rest,
For none are wholly free from sin;
And they who fain would serve thee best
Are conscious most of wrong within.

O Saviour Christ, thou too art man;
Thou hast been troubled, tempted, tried;
Thy kind but searching glance can scan
The very wounds that shame would hide;

Thy word has still its ancient power;
No word from thee can fruitless fall:
Hear in this solemn evening hour,
And, in thy mercy, heal us all.

H. Twells (1823–1900)

August has always been a great month for celebrations. The Guards fife and drum band turns up outside the home of our dearly loved Queen Elizabeth, the Queen Mother, each August to play "Happy Birthday to You!" And bell-ringers ring special peals from church towers across the land. The Queen Mother is as old as the century. Fifty years later, in the same month, Princess Anne, the Princess Royal, was born, so she will be celebrating her fiftieth birthday the year we begin the next century.

A little less grandly, we used to celebrate my brother Neville's birthday in August, and nowadays our grandson James has his on 13 August. The month ends with a bank holiday weekend (well it does in England and Wales), the last holiday of the year, before Christmas.

Now, how would you expect 20,000 youngsters to spend it, if they were all together? Behaving badly? Running wild? May I suggest that you take a trip up (or down, as the case may be) the M1, to somewhere in the Midlands next August? Join more than that number of young people at a huge camp site, for an event known as Greenbelt, where every year they spend the three days of the bank holiday weekend at religious workshops, studying the Bible, listening to Christian speakers, worshipping together, talking, arguing, dancing, clowning, and, above all, making very loud music indeed!

I haven't been along myself – well, I don't think Scotty and I are quite the right age group – but we have watched *Songs of Praise* from Greenbelt, and I included a big part of it on **Praise Be!** one year. And I'm here to tell you, those young people are smashing!

If young people don't want to come along to church – and many of them seem to feel that traditional church services, which we older people love, are not for them – I don't think it's because they aren't interested in religion. But there is the generation gap. Young people like different radio stations, different television programmes, they have different fashions in clothes, dances, music – different everything. Are you surprised that they want to have their own words and music to express their ideas about Jesus?

When I was in the Big Top at Minehead one Spring, talking to Graham Kendrick, the hymn writer whose hymns have been taken up very enthusiastically by young Christians, he said:

"I think it would be a tragedy if no new songs were written, because worship is an overflow of a relationship with God, and if a new generation is discovering God for themselves, they're going to sing about it. So it's a sign of life. And after all, the old favourites were once new, and when they were new, they were criticized. It even happened to Charles Wesley. He used tunes from operettas, which was considered very worldly!"

Graham also said: "The important thing is to make sure that actually we are worshipping God, and not just having a little nostalgic trip." And so say I.

Here's one of Graham's hymns which I'm always being asked for on **Praise Be!** – by young and old!

Lord, The Light of Your Love Is Shining

Lord, the light of your love is shining
In the midst of the darkness shining;
Jesus, Light of the world, shine upon us,
Set us free by the truth you now bring us,
Shine on me, shine on me.

Shine, Jesus, shine,
Fill the land with the Father's glory;
Blaze, Spirit, blaze,
Set our hearts on fire.
Flow, river, flow,
Flood the nations with grace and mercy;
Send forth your word, Lord
And let there be light.

Lord, I come to your awesome presence,
From the shadows into your radiance;
By the blood I may enter your brightness,
Search me, try me, consume all my darkness.
Shine on me, shine on me.

As we gaze on your kingly brightness
So our faces display your likeness,
Ever changing from glory to glory,
Mirrored here may our lives tell your story,
Shine on me, shine on me.

Shine, Jesus, shine,
Fill the land with Father's glory;
Blaze, Spirit, blaze,
Set our hearts on fire,

Flow, river, flow,
Flood the nations with grace and mercy;
Send forth your word, Lord
And let there be light.

Graham Kendrick (1988)

September

Come, ye thankful people, come,
Raise the song of harvest-home:
All is safely gathered in,
Ere the winter storms begin;
God, our Maker, doth provide
For our wants to be supplied:
Come to God's own temple, come,
Raise the song of harvest-home.

from "Come, ye thankful people, come"
by Henry Alford (1819–71)

Just as I was sitting here wondering what I wanted to say about September, the bells started ringing in a nearby church. It must be their practice night. I love the sound of church bells, don't you? They seem to gather the whole town together. It has always been my proud boast that they were ringing on the morning I was born – but only because I was born on a Sunday!

But these bells pealing away now – Bob Major or Grandsire Triples or whatever it is they are ringing – have brought back to my mind the war years, and the Battle of Britain, in September 1940.

Anyone who was harvesting in the fields, orchards and hop gardens of Kent that year had a ringside seat for that terrible battle in the September sky. I received a letter one year from a lady from the East End of London, who remembered everybody sitting under the trees to pick the hops off the vines and gather them into the baskets, while the planes battled to and fro over their heads, and someone started singing "The Old Rugged Cross."

We all thought that Hitler would invade Britain. It was agreed that the warning, if there was an invasion, would be for all the church bells to be rung (they had all been silenced for the duration of the war). If they had been used to ring out this warning, every single person in Britain would have been able to hear them, because we have enough churches with bell-towers and ringers, to reach every corner of the land. And you never know, that still might come in useful one day.

Now birth and death-reminding bells ring clear,
Loud under 'planes and over changing gear.

John Betjeman

It still *feels* like summer in September, but in the early mornings it sometimes looks as though someone has hung out very delicate net curtains along the hedgerows – dew-covered spiders' webs sparkling and gleaming in the morning sun. For me, that's always the first sign that autumn is on the way.

Early in September the sky is full of swallows and house-martins, flying low round the house checking all the eaves and nesting places to round up the late families. Then one day we go outside, and realize that they are missing. We won't see any of them again before St George's Day the following April. I go back indoors only to find, looking expectantly in at me through the kitchen window, eight or nine members of a slightly less welcome visitor – daddy-long-legs! Weren't there a lot last year?

I rather think that I see more of our garden hedgehog around the place in September, too. As the rosy sun-set creeps imperceptibly earlier and earlier each evening, he seems to be more preoccupied than usual. I think he's busy building up a big fat tummy to last him through his winter hibernation under the compost heap. Anyway, it's jolly to see him trundling about, and I sometimes ask Scotty to put out a saucer of dog-food for him on a chilly night.

All Creatures of Our God and King

All creatures of our God and King,
Lift up your voice and with us sing
Allelulia, alleluia!
Thou burning sun with golden beam,
Thou silver moon with softer gleam,
O praise him, O praise him,
Alleluia, alleluia, alleluia!

Thou rushing wind that art so strong,
Ye clouds that sail in heaven along,
O praise him, alleluia!
Thou rising morn, in praise rejoice,
Ye lights of evening, find a voice;
O praise him, O praise him,
Alleluia, alleluia, alleluia!

Thou flowing water, pure and clear,
Make music for thy Lord to hear,
Alleluia, alleluia!
Thou fire, so masterful and bright,
That givest man both warmth and light,
O praise him, O praise him,
Alleluia, alleluia, alleluia!

Dear mother earth, who day by day
Unfoldest blessings on our way,
O praise him, alleluia!
The flowers and fruits that in thee grow,
Let them his glory also show;
O praise him, O praise him,
Alleluia, alleluia, alleluia!

And all ye men of tender heart,
Forgiving others, take your part,
O sing ye, alleluia!
Ye who long pain and sorrow bear,
Praise God and on him cast your care;
O praise him, O praise him,
Alleluia, alleluia, alleluia!

And thou, most kind and gentle death,
Waiting to hush our latest breath,
O praise him, alleluia!
Thou leadest home the child of God,
And Christ our Lord the way hath trod;
O praise him, O praise him,
Alleluia, alleluia, alleluia!

Let all things their Creator bless,
And worship him in humbleness;

O praise him, alleluia!
Praise, praise the Father, praise the Son,
And praise the Spirit, Three in One;
O praise him, O praise him,
Alleluia, alleluia, alleluia!

W. H. Draper (1855–1933)
Based on St Francis of Assisi's
Canticle of the Sun

In the countryside farmers, villagers and "church mice" are all preparing for Harvest Home. The Harvest Supper Committee are working out how to serve a hundred hot suppers in a village hall with no cooking facilities. Someone is out collecting raffle prizes, and also looking for volunteers to help with the washing up – so supper won't have to be served on paper plates and eaten with plastic knives and forks!

What a Saturday night it will be! There will be cider and punch to drink, and to eat: baked potatoes and hot stew, salad and cheese, followed by apple pie and cream – and all home-made. Delicious! Every table will be decorated with beautiful arrangements of fruit and flowers. The vicar will say grace, and supper will be followed by the raffle draw, then the entertainers and a sing-song. It's a cheerful, well-deserved annual get-together for a hard-working community.

Meanwhile, the "church mice" – who give so much of their time and skill all year, keeping our churches dusted and polished and bright with flowers – are as busy as can be creating wonderful arrangements with chrysanthemums, dahlias, daisies and autumn leaves, while the church around them steadily fills with offerings of gigantic marrows, prize-winning parsnips, carrots, tomatoes, apples, pears, grapes, eggs, honey, marmalade, barley loaves and wheatsheaves. Town and city churches are not out-done: they take home-made jams, tins of meat and fruit and vegetables, torch batteries, home-made candles and hand-knitted scarves and mittens along to their altars. All these gifts, from town and country, will be given to hospitals, nursing homes and local elderly people after the Harvest Festival Service.

> If not now – when?
> If not us – who?
>
> chanted on a March for Jesus,
> (September 1990)

Did you happen to watch *Songs of Praise* from Leeds Castle, in Kent, in September 1990, on Battle of Britain Sunday? There were thousands of young people on the programme, who had all been on a "March for Jesus", and in between the songs, they spoke a lot of good sense. The "March for Jesus" is quite a new annual event which perhaps one day will become as familiar as the Harvest Festival. It takes place in towns and cities up and down the country. It's very joyful and absolutely chaotic, with thousands of people milling about with balloons and banners and banging drums. They call it the *New* Battle of Britain – and they are telling everyone about Jesus, and what he can do for every single person in the world. For all the Christian churches the last ten years of the second millennium is to be, I quote, "a Decade of evangelism – making Christ known to the people of his world". And like all those people on a "March for Jesus",

we can all help. How? Well ask yourself the same
question they did:

> If not now – when?
> If not us – who?

God is Working His Purpose Out

God is working his purpose out
  as year succeeds to year,
God is working his purpose out,
  and the time is drawing near;
Nearer and nearer draws the time,
  the time that shall surely be,
When the earth shall be filled with the glory of God
  as the waters cover the sea.

From utmost east to utmost west
  where'er man's foot has trod,
By the mouth of many messengers
  goes forth the voice of God,
"Give ear to me, ye continents,
  ye isles, give ear to me,
That the earth shall be filled with the glory of God
  as the waters cover the sea."

What can we do to work God's work,
  to prosper and increase
The brotherhood of all mankind,
  the reign of the Prince of Peace?
What can we do to hasten the time,
  the time that shall surely be,

When the earth shall be filled with the glory of God
  as the waters cover the sea.

March we forth in the strength of God
  with the Banner of Christ unfurled,
That the light of the glorious gospel of truth
  may shine throughout the world.
Fight we the fight with sorrow and sin,
  to set their captives free,
That the earth shall be filled with the glory of God
  as the waters cover the sea.

All we can do is nothing worth
  unless God blesses the deed;
Vainly we hope for the harvest-tide
  till God gives life to the seed;
Yet nearer and nearer draws the time,
  the time that shall surely be,
When the earth shall be filled with the glory of God
  as the waters cover the sea.

A. C. Ainger (1841–1919)

Autumn

Do you like marigolds?
Here's a pledge
To meet the frost with
A golden edge –

To go as far as
A weak thing may
Linking to-morrow with
Yesterday.

from Marigolds, by Louis Driscoll
    in *The Golden Staircase* (Nelson)

October

Hours fly, flowers die, love stays

words written on an old sundial

On every tall tree there's a robin or a thrush or a blackbird giving us a solo performance. It's as if they understand that we're feeling a bit melancholy, summer is over and the swallows and martins have left us for another year. Silent all summer, our faithful little native birds pour their hearts out in the October sunset, haunting autumn songs, quite different from spring's cacophonous dawn chorus.

Blackpool illuminations are one thing, but for Scotty and me the real treat in October is to go out for a drive in the Sussex Weald countryside, to see the trees in their autumn colours. There was one road in particular which we always used to travel along each October, on the way to Benenden, where Daisy was at school. It's long and straight, and it was lined with huge arching beech trees. As we drove through this bright gold avenue each autumn, we would say to one another: "Oh! It's like being in a cathedral."

Then came the gales of October 1987, and nearly every tree fell.

They've planted new ones, and in twenty years' time I hope other families will go driving along there, as Scotty and I have done so often, and turn to one another and say: "It's like being in a cathedral."

Do you ever get that feeling, you know, when you see something so beautiful in nature, that you should take off your shoes, because it is holy ground?

> The angel of the Lord appeared unto Moses in a flame of fire out of the midst of a bush: and he looked, and behold, the bush burned with fire, and the bush was not consumed.
>
> And Moses said, "I will now turn aside, and see this great sight, why the bush is not burnt."
>
> And when the Lord saw that he turned aside to see, God called unto him out of the midst of the bush, and said, "Moses, Moses."
>
> And he said, "Here am I."
>
> And he said, "Draw not nigh hither: put off thy shoes from off thy feet, for the place whereon thou standest is holy ground."
>
> Exodus 3:2–5 (AV)

Some churches have an Animal's Service at the beginning of October, on the nearest Sunday to the 4th, the feast of St Francis of Assisi. Everyone brings along their family pets. What an assembly! And what a cacophony, when the service begins! There's always a ginger tom that really doesn't like any of the other animals. The hymns are all accompanied by barking dogs, mewing cats, the rustling of mice and hamsters peering anxiously from their straw-filled boxes; bantam hens cluck disapprovingly at their neighbour's angora rabbits, goldfish swim sadly round and round their "cars" (special small bowls for transporting fish) . . . you even have people bringing goats, sheep, pigs, donkeys and ponies! The blessing by the Vicar, and Oh dear! – before there's time for everyone to respond ''Amen'', there's a rabbit on the loose under the front pew, and two old mongrels are announcing their dislike of one another in front of the whole congregation.

Jan's always loved animals, and she has quite a menagerie. I always remember when Tess, Jan's golden labrador, had puppies – one of whom was Patch, whom she kept, and you've seen them both on **Praise Be!** Now these puppies were crosses, you understand, not exactly mongrels, but not priceless pedigree pooches either. But if you had wanted one, you would have thought you must be buying the most important puppy in the world! Jan put all prospective new owners through a stern and rigorous examination – what sort of house do you live in? How big is the garden? Are you out all day working? How often will you take him or her for walks? – before she would let any of her treasures go.

St Francis is probably the best known and best loved of all the saints – his famous love of animals makes him an especial favourite with children. I heard Norman St John Stevas say on television the other day that St Francis did not write the beautiful prayer for peace called The Prayer of St Francis, and that it was written – oh, I can't remember by whom or when he said, but much later. I hope he's not right, but be that as it may, I'm quite sure that it was *inspired* by St Francis.

The Prayer of St Francis

Lord, make me an instrument of your peace.
Where there is hatred, let me sow love,
Where there is injury, pardon;
Where there is doubt, faith;
Where there is despair, hope;
Where there is darkness, light;
Where there is sadness, joy.
O divine Master,
Grant that I may not so much seek
To be consoled as to console,
To be understood, as to understand,
To be loved, as to love,
For it is in giving that we receive;
It is in pardoning that we are pardoned;
It is in dying that we are born to eternal life.

A little later, on 18 October, it's St Luke's Tide, when Christians pray for all doctors and nurses and medical people. And I owe them such a lot particularly after my last stay in hospital for a heart by-pass. What an amazing operation! I'm so very grateful to everybody for the care they took of me.

I sometimes think: if only they'd known how to do all this when my mother was alive, she wouldn't have died aged sixty-two. But it's no good being anything but thankful for the advances they've made and are making all the time. And so, as the old lady said when she was asked the secret of a long happy life: ''I goes to bed 'opeful, and I wakes up thankful!''

I also wake early. I'm not one of those who likes it when the clocks go back in October. I've never enjoyed lying in, and it usually means we're up and about at five in the morning for a few days, instead of six, until our systems re-adjust. I think many people over sixty find themselves waking up early in the mornings. It's one of the good things about getting older, and you'd be surprised how much you can get done first thing, before anyone else is up. I learn words, and I know one lady who does her baking early in the mornings, and her lucky neighbours often wake up to find a gift of hot, freshly baked bread rolls on their doorsteps.

Did you know that before the coming of the railways there was no standard time in different parts of the country? So it could be seven o'clock in Reading and say, twenty past seven in Tunbridge Wells? Every area worked the time out for themselves according to the sun, and it wasn't until they needed to write train timetables that they realized they had better agree what time it really was! Not a lot of people know that . . .

There are very few mornings when I don't see the dawn come in. I feel I have the world to myself for half an hour.

When Morning Gilds the Skies

When morning gilds the skies,
My heart awaking cries,
May Jesus Christ be praised:
Alike at work and prayer

To Jesus I repair;
May Jesus Christ be praised.

Whene'er the sweet church bell
Peals over hill and dell,
May Jesus Christ be praised:
O hark to what it sings,
As joyously it rings,
'May Jesus Christ be praised.

My tongue shall never tire
Of chanting with the choir,
May Jesus Christ be praised:
This song of sacred joy,
It never seems to cloy,
May Jesus Christ be praised.

Does sadness fill my mind?
A solace here I find,
May Jesus Christ be praised:
Or fades my earthly bliss?
My comfort still is this,
May Jesus Christ be praised.

Be this, while life is mine,
My canticle divine,
May Jesus Christ be praised:
Be this the eternal song
Through ages all along,
May Jesus Christ be praised.

Trs from German by
E. Caswall (1874–78)

In the old Celtic calendar, and in the pagan world, the last night of October was "old year night", the night when all the witches were said to be abroad, malevolently exercising their magic powers. Even though the Church transformed it into the Eve of All Saints, Hallowe'en has never quite shaken off its associations with witchcraft.

Children immensely enjoy rushing round at Hallowe'en dressed as little demons, demanding their Trick or Treat, but the pagan side of things can get out of hand sometimes. Our part of rural Sussex has become quite notorious in recent years because of stories about witches and black magic and nasty things going bump in the night. Most of it is just people enjoying telling a scary tale, but they start to believe it themselves and then they convince other people, and before you know where you are, we're back in the Middle Ages.

Fortunately we have the wonderful Bishop Peter Ball as our Suffragen Bishop of Lewes, one of the twin brothers who are both monks and both bishops. He helps us see things the right way round. He is a great walker, and loves walking for miles all over the Sussex Downs. Someone said to him: "Aren't you ever nervous, Bishop Peter, walking about on your own in such remote places, when there are such funny goings on?" He answered: "Nervous? On my own? Why, there are so many angels about, I have to push them to one side to get along the lane!"

Psalm 23

The Lord is my shepherd; I shall not want.

He maketh me to lie down in green pastures: he leadeth me beside the still waters.

He restoreth my soul: he leadeth me in the paths of righteousness for his name's sake.

Yea, though I walk through the valley of the shadow of death, I will fear no evil: for thou art with me; thy rod and thy staff they comfort me.

Thou preparest a table before me in the presence of mine enemies: thou anointest my head with oil; my cup runneth over.

Surely goodness and mercy shall follow me all the days of my life; and I will dwell in the house of the Lord for ever.

Psalm 23 (AV)

November

Part of the service in our parish church is the "collect of the day", the special prayer which has been prayed on that particular Sunday every year since medieval times. I suppose they would have been in Latin originally. As the years go by, you get to know some of them by heart, because you hear them so often, and they are mostly very short, simple and profound. One of my favourites comes towards the end of November:

Stir up, we beseech thee, O Lord, the wills of thy faithful people; that they, plenteously bringing forth the fruit of good works, may of thee be plenteously rewarded; through Jesus Christ our Lord.

Amen

Collect for the Twenty-fifth Sunday after Trinity (BCP)

We call it "Stir-up" Sunday, don't you, the week we have this prayer? Because it always comes as such a timely reminder to make the Christmas pudding. Well – look at the words again, if you don't believe me!

When I was young, Neville and I took turns cutting the stones out of the big raisins. It was a terrible job. You got so sticky and got more on your fingers than into the bowl. So many things are easier now, like seedless fruit. Then we all had to take turns stirring the Christmas pudding mixture, because you really had to stir and stir

for hours. We used to make it in the basin part of a jug
and basin set. I remember standing on the chair by the
kitchen table holding the wooden spoon with two hands,
trying to heave the mixture round the huge bowl – and
taking deep sniffs of the heady aroma from the cinnamon
and barley wine and rum. Mmm, I can smell it now!

November begins with All Saints Day, and if your church
is called "All Saints" I expect you fill it with white daisies
and lilies on 1 November, ring out the bells, and have
a wonderful celebration!

Men and women who have lived very holy lives are
made Saints, and it's right to respect them and learn from
their example. But what's also nice is that Jesus chose his
friends and followers from among the holy muddle of
ordinary people. Very often he seems to have preferred
people who were rather less than perfect, rough
diamonds to say the least. But they are all Saints now.
So I like to think that he calls everyone who loves him
his "saints"!

As that great jazz number, which I told Sue Lawley I
would take with me to my Desert Island, goes:

> When the saints go marching in,
> When the saints go marching in,
> Lord, I want to be in that number
> When the saints go marching in!

Churches are full on Remembrance Sunday, but the annual two minutes' silence used to be taken far more seriously than it is today. I remember how long it always seemed, when we stood in line at school. I thought it was an hour. Everyone stopped whatever they were doing at the eleventh hour of the eleventh day of the eleventh month – and it didn't matter if it was a busy week-day. All the traffic would stop at eleven o'clock. Even the bus drivers would climb out of their cabs and stand on the pavement with bared heads to keep the two minutes' silence.

Nowadays, if you are in church keeping the silence on the nearest Sunday, it is quite probably being interrupted with yells and shouts from a football match going on outside, or the roar of the traffic. I think it's a shame. Young people are still giving thier lives for our country. I think we let them down badly if we don't keep faith with them.

Because the Royal Family played such an important part in keeping up our spirits during the Second World War, some older people prefer to spend Remembrance Sunday with the Queen – well, watching the televised ceremony at the Cenotaph, anyway! Scotty and I do, and the highlight always for us is the march past of all the wonderful old veterans and Chelsea Pensioners, while the band strikes up "We are the boys of the Old Brigade . . ." Oh dear! Off I go again. Not a dry eye in our front room!

Here's a hymn for Remembrance Sunday that not many of us can get through without having to blow our noses!

O Valiant Hearts

O valiant hearts, who to your glory came
Through dust of conflict and through battle flame;
Tranquil you lie, your knightly virtue proved,
Your memory hallowed in the land you loved.

Proudly you gathered, rank on rank, to war,
As who had heard God's message from afar;
All you had hoped for, all you had, you gave
To save mankind – yourselves you scorned to save.

Long years ago, as earth lay dark and still,
Rose a loud cry upon a lonely hill,
While in the frailty of our human clay
Christ, our Redeemer, passed the self-same way.

Still stands his Cross from that dread hour to this,
Like some bright star above the dark abyss;
Still, through the veil, the Victor's pitying eyes
Look down to bless our lesser Calvaries.

O risen Lord, O Shepherd of our dead,
Whose Cross has brought them and whose staff has led,
In glorious hope, their proud and sorrowing land
Commits her children to thy gracious hand.

Sir John S. Arkwright

I don't want to offend anyone, but our family are not great ones for the tradition of burning effigies of Guy Fawkes on November the fifth, although it's a big occasion in our nearest town. Over 30,000 people crowd into Lewes, and one year *Songs of Praise* even came from there. I know they aren't harming anybody, but I have to confess it always makes me feel a little bit uncomfortable.

But we do have plenty of garden bonfires in November. As the month goes by all the golden leaves, so beautiful on the trees, start to drop and quickly turn into brown mud on the grass, so they all have to be raked up. Scotty puts loads of them into plastic sacks to make leaf mould, and the rest we burn on bonfires made up of weeds, dead hollyhocks and stuff, hedge-cuttings, pruned-off branches of fruit trees and roses, and all the things like that.

I love the November smell of bonfire smoke in the frosty air. Did you know that the word "bonfire" was originally "bone" fire? People couldn't afford to feed their sheep and cattle all through the winter, so in the autumn they would kill large numbers of them, and burn the carcases on bone fires. Yes, I know. Horrid!

Though we "pass" on Guy Fawkes, we're always invited by Jan and William to a Thanksgiving Dinner, with a lot of their American friends, because Jan is married to our favourite American, William! So Thanksgiving has become a family tradition. You'll find us eating things like toasted marshmallows, yams, sweet potatoes and pumpkin pie (made from pumpkins grown in the garden – you should have seen the size of them this year. Phew!). And as we always enjoy a traditional turkey for the Thanksgiving dinner, we have goose at Christmas.

Now Thank We All Our God

Now thank we all our God,
With hearts and hands and voices,
Who wondrous things hath done,
In whom his world rejoices;
Who from our mother's arms
Hath blessed us on our way
With countless gifts of love,
And still is ours today.

O may this bounteous God
Through all our life be near us,
With ever joyful hearts
And blessed peace to cheer us;
And keep us in his grace,
And guide us when perplexed,
And free us from all ills
In this world and the next.

All praise and thanks to God
The Father now be given,
The Son, and him who reigns
With them in highest heaven,
The one eternal God,
Whom earth and heaven adore,
For thus it was, is now,
And shall be evermore.

M. Rinkart (1586–1649)
Tr. Catherine Winkworth

November ends with St Andrew's Day, patron saint of Scotland, where my Scotty hails from. We haven't been up for a year or two now, but we've taken the high road, and the low road, to Forfar on many a spring and autumn holiday, and we spent our honeymoon there, so you might know, Scotland has a special place in our hearts.

Jesus Calls Us!

Jesus calls us! Oe'er the tumult
Of our life's wild restless sea,
Day by day his sweet voice soundeth,
Saying, "Christian, follow me":

As of old, Saint Andrew heard it
By the Galilean lake,
Turned from home, and toil, and kindred,
Leaving all for his dear sake.

Jesus calls us from the worship
Of the vain world's golden store,
From each idol that would keep us,
Saying, "Christian, love me more."

In our joys and in our sorrows,
Days of toil and hours of ease,
Still he calls, in cares and pleasures,
"Christians, love me more than these."

Jesus calls us! By thy mercies,
Saviour, may we hear thy call,
Give our hearts to thy obedience,
Serve and love thee best of all.

Mrs C. F. Alexander (1818–95)

P.S.!

Out in the orchard I can see a million starlings descending on the remains of the pears that were left unpicked and have started to rot. They give off a heady smell when you walk past. And that reminds me, as November draws to a close, I really must go and help Scotty "stir up" the fruit of good works that have gone into our Christmas pudding!

Advent

When you come to the last page of your calendar, that's when the Christian year begins. It's a topsy-turvy old world! But this is the true beginning of the story of Jesus, the time of Advent and Christmas.

What we call the beginning is often the end
And to make an end is to make a beginning.
The end is where we start from.

T. S. Eliot – "Little Gidding"

December

This year in our church we had a Christingle Service at the beginning of December. Oh, if only we'd had a camera there to film the children! There were forty-three of them, not one of them over the age of three or four, and they each carried an orange tied round with a red ribbon, with a candle stuck in it. They carried them, you know how children do, right under their chins. And one little girl, who wore a dress like a Victorian Christmas card, kept escaping from her mother and going to look at the Advent wreath at the front. Oh, I wish you could have been there. It was all beautiful.

Do you know what a "christingle" is, by the way? I didn't either! But here's a song that tells you.

The Christingle Song

It's rounded like an orange,
This earth on which we stand
And we praise the God who holds it
In the hollow of his hand.

So, Father, we would thank you,
For all that you have done,
And for all that you have given us
Through the coming of your Son.

A candle burning brightly
Can cheer the darkest night,
And these candles tell how Jesus
Came to bring a dark world light.

The ribbon round the orange
Reminds us of the cost;
How the Shepherd, strong and gentle,
Gave his life to save the lost.

We come with our Christingles
To tell of Jesus' birth
And we praise the God who blessed us
By his coming to this earth.

So, Father, we would thank you,
For all that you have done,
And for all that you have given us
Through the coming of your Son.

Christmas is coming
The goose is getting fat
Please put a penny in the old man's hat?
If you haven't got a penny,
A ha'penny will do.
If you haven't got a ha'penny,
God bless you!

Christmas always arrives sooner than I expect and before
I'm ready, and we also have two December birthdays in
the family: Jan was born on December 14, and Daisy was
born in America on December 13. Because of the time

difference, when Jan telephoned on December 13 to tell us Daisy had arrived, the first thing we said to her was "Happy birthday, darling!" Well, you see, in England it was already December 14!

It's sometimes difficult to know what to give a person whose birthday comes so close to Christmas, and we have toyed with the idea of having an "official" birthday for Daisy, like the Queen, in June. Until we get round to announcing the date, there's nothing I enjoy more than taking Daisy to the theatre in December for a birthday treat.

If I'm looking for something a bit different for friends, as often as not it will have come from an open-air market. I'm a person who finds it very hard to pass a market without stopping to have a good poke round. I like the sights and sounds – you know, like those men who hurl twenty plates in the air and catch them and say, "I'm not offering them to you for fifty pounds, ladies . . . I'm not offering them for forty. Not thirty. Not twenty. But fifteen pounds! Ladies and gentlemen! Fifteen pounds! I ask you. I'm robbing myself, I know, but just call me Father Christmas . . ." That's as much pleasure for me as buying the things they sell, although I've picked up a few little treasures in my time!

There are so many wonderful carol services to go to in December, and I always want to be at them all! I never manage it, but I try very hard not to miss the Ancient Order of Foresters Carol Service at Westminster Hall, or the Salvation Army Carol Service in their Regent Street Citadel.

That's always extra special for me, because it brings

back happy memories of the Salvation Army Band playing carols, standing in the middle of Cheapside every Christmas.

Sometimes I'm invited to read part of the Christmas story – and they are such loving people, they always applaud at the end! And I'm here to tell you, no one can sing Christmas songs and carols like that huge gathering of Salvation Army officers.

I've been a lifelong admirer of the Sally-Ann, and all the work they do, especially for people who are down and out, and whom no one else wants to help. At Christmas many a homeless wanderer at the end of their tether is welcomed in to their hostels and given friendship, warmth, music and a turkey dinner.

A cry in the night
And a child is born;
A child in a stable,
There isn't any room:
A cry in the night, and God has made
Our homelessness his home.

From "Ballad of the Homeless Christ"
by Geoff Ainger (b. 1925)

Christmas Day

Joy to the World

Joy to the world! the Lord is come;
Let earth receive her King;
Let every heart prepare him room,
And heaven and nature sing,
And heaven and nature sing,
And heaven, and heaven and nature sing.

Joy to the world! the Saviour reigns;
Let us our songs employ;
While fields and floods, rocks, hills and plains,
Repeat the sounding joy,
Repeat the sounding joy,
Repeat, repeat the sounding joy.

No more let sin and sorrow grow,
Nor thorns infest the ground;
He comes to make his blessings flow
Far as the curse is found,
Far as the curse is found,
Far as, far as the curse is found.

He rules the world with truth and grace,
And makes the nations prove
The glories of his righteousness,
And wonders of his love,
And wonders of his love,
And wonders, and wonders of his love.

Isaac Watts (1683–1748)

Christmas is such a special time, that I think I'm going to have a go at my own little book for Christmas. Do you think you will like it?

Another thing I have always wanted to do is to present a special Christmas Day edition of **Praise Be!** I would share Christmas with the many people who are on their own. It would be great. We would have all our favourite Christmas music and talk about memories of happy days, and the time would just fly by. Perhaps, like my ride in the donkey cart, this wish too will come true one day! You never know. Whether it does or not, may I wish you all a very happy and blessed Christmas.

And is it true? And is it true,
This most tremendous tale of all,
Seen in a stained-glass window's hue,
A Baby in an ox's stall?
The Maker of the stars and sea
Become a Child on earth for me?

And is it true? For if it is,
No loving fingers tying strings
Around those tissued fripperies,
The sweet and silly Christmas things,
Bath salts and inexpensive scent
And hideous tie so kindly meant,

No love that in a family dwells,
No carolling in frosty air,
Nor all the steeple-shaking bells
Can with this single truth compare –
That God was Man in Palestine
And lives today in Bread and Wine.

from "Christmas" by John Betjeman

P.S.
And a happy New Year!
Now turn back to page one, please!